Praise for

Strangers at My Door

"*Strangers at My Door* is not only an invitation into the life of a hospitality house; it's an invitation into real Christianity. By that I mean the radical inclusivity of Jesus that embraces and fights for the ones mainstream society shuns and abhors and terminates without batting an eye. It is, in short, an invitation for each of us to open our lives to the stranger and become more fully human."

—SISTER HELEN PREJAN, author of *Dead Man Walking*

"We Franciscans are always happy and impressed when other folks discover what we were supposed to be known for! The Franciscan 'charism' never dies and always re-emerges in fresh form—because it is the very 'marrow of the Gospel'. Jonathan Wilson-Hartgrove is teaching you how to live that Gospel in our time, and in such fresh and alive ways."

—FR. RICHARD ROHR, OFM, academic dean of the Living School for Action and Contemplation, Center for Action and Contemplation

"Fifty years ago, when the Civil Rights movement came to Mississippi, I saw the wisdom of the approach that says, 'Go to the people. Live with them. Learn from them.' Those young people did what Jesus had done, and black folks from the South were able to change America and say, 'We've done it ourselves.' Jonathan and his friends at Rutba House have joined that same quiet revolution, and they are not alone. They give me hope that America may yet be born again."

—JOHN M. PERKINS, founder of the Christian
Community Development Association

"With elegant prose honed by brutal honesty, Jonathan Wilson-Hartgrove provides a theological account of what it means to welcome the stranger—strangers who often turn out to lack any gratitude. Wilson-Hartgrove's narrative gives one hope as he refuses to be defeated by ungratefulness."

—STANLEY HAUERWAS, Gilbert T. Rowe Professor of
Theological Ethics at Duke University

"Jonathan is a dear friend and brother and a partner in holy mischief. *Strangers at My Door* invites you to eavesdrop on a radical faith community as it practices one of the most fundamental Christian distinctives—welcoming the stranger. Jonathan invites you to join this movement of Christians who want to be known more for who we have embraced than who we have excluded."

—SHANE CLAIBORNE, activist and author of *Jesus for
President* and *The Irresistible Revolution*

strangers at
my door

"I was a stranger and you welcomed me." —Jesus

strangers at my door

A TRUE STORY OF FINDING JESUS IN UNEXPECTED GUESTS

Jonathan Wilson-Hartgrove

CONVERGENT

BOOKS

STRANGERS AT MY DOOR
PUBLISHED BY CONVERGENT BOOKS

All Scripture quotations, unless otherwise indicated, are taken from the Holy Bible, New International Version®, NIV®. Copyright © 1973, 1978, 1984, 2011 by Biblica Inc.™ Used by permission of Zondervan. All rights reserved worldwide. www.zondervan.com. Scripture quotations marked (ESV) are taken from The Holy Bible, English Standard Version, copyright © 2001 by Crossway Bibles, a division of Good News Publishers. Used by permission. All rights reserved. Scripture quotations marked (KJV) are taken from the King James Version. Scripture quotations marked (NLT) are taken from the Holy Bible, New Living Translation, copyright © 1996, 2004, 2007. Used by permission of Tyndale House Publishers Inc., Carol Stream, Illinois 60188. All rights reserved.

Grateful acknowledgment is made for the use of "Easter Morning" from *The Way It Is: New and Selected Poems* by William Stafford, copyright © 1998 by the Estate of William Stafford. Reprinted with the permission of The Permissions Company Inc., on behalf of Graywolf Press, Minneapolis, Minnesota. www.graywolfpress.org.

Details in some anecdotes and stories have been changed to protect the identities of the persons involved.

Trade Paperback ISBN 978-0-307-73195-1
eBook ISBN 978-0-307-73196-8

Copyright © 2013 by Jonathan Wilson-Hartgrove

Cover design by Tim Green, FaceOut Studio; cover photography by Getty Images

Published in the United States by Convergent, an imprint of the Crown Publishing Group, a division of Random House LLC, New York, a Penguin Random House Company.

CONVERGENT BOOKS and its open book colophon are trademarks of Random House LLC.

Library of Congress Cataloging-in-Publication Data
  Wilson-Hartgrove, Jonathan, 1980–
    Strangers at my door : a true story of finding Jesus in unexpected guests / Jonathan Wilson-Hartgrove.
      pages cm
  ISBN 978-0-307-73195-1 (pbk.) — ISBN 978-0-307-73196-8 (electronic)
    1. Hospitality—Religious aspects—Christianity. I. Title.
  BV4647.H67W55 2013
  241'.671—dc23

2013018874

Printed in the United States of America
2013—First Edition

10 9 8 7 6 5 4 3 2 1

SPECIAL SALES
Most Convergent books are available at special quantity discounts when purchased in bulk by corporations, organizations, and special-interest groups. Custom imprinting or excerpting can also be done to fit special needs. For information, please e-mail Special Markets@ConvergentBooks.com or call 1-800-603-7051.

For Leah, who knows why—or should

I was a stranger, and you invited me into your home.

—Jesus (Matthew 25:35, NLT)

Contents

Judgment Day

The house is cold at midnight, so I put on slippers before going downstairs. Everyone else has gone to bed, including my son, whose asthma was complicated tonight by a cold. I tiptoe across the hardwood floor, careful not to wake anyone, and take a drinking glass from the cabinet. But before I turn on the faucet, I hear the shuffle of feet at the door.

Knock, knock.

Whoever is standing outside, I know, can read the words of Jesus engraved on our door knocker: "I was a stranger and you welcomed me." The visitor who is knocking probably has heard the story about how my wife, Leah, and I were part of a peacemaker delegation in 2003. We visited Iraq at the time of America's intensive bombing campaign. On a desolate desert road, our friends were nearly killed when their driver lost control after hitting a chunk of shrapnel in the road. But some locals picked them up and took them to the doctor in a town called Rutba.

"Three days ago," the doctor said, "your country bombed our hospital. But we will take care of you."

Literally by accident, we lived a modern-day Good Samaritan story. The Good Iraqi—the Good Muslim—showed us what God's love looks like. When we heard Jesus say, "Go and do likewise" at the end of that gospel story, we knew it was an invitation to practice the love we had received. So we named this place Rutba House. We put a knocker by the front door that bears Jesus's statement about being a welcomed Stranger. We invited folks who were homeless to consider this their home.

For a decade now, they have. They have come here after fleeing abusive partners, and they've come straight from prison—sometimes for a night, sometimes for life. They've shown up scared by the trauma of war abroad and haunted by the horrors of violence in homes that fell apart. They've been drug dealers who wanted a fresh start, lifelong addicts who needed a place to die, kids whose families had come undone, street workers who wanted to sit down and eat a sandwich. They've brought with them a universe that's every bit as broken as that bombed-out highway in the Iraqi desert.

They come here with pressing needs, and they have taught me hope. I believe in the miracle of Rutba, and not just because I lived it in the desert of Iraq. I've seen the miracle repeated time and again, right here in my home. A knock comes at our door, and we are saved.

"This being human is a guest house," wrote the Sufi poet Rumi. We are, each of us, a hospitality house of sorts. We go about our daily lives on busy streets, often strapped to a piece of steel moving at forty miles per hour. But even if it's through a car window with the doors locked, our eyes connect with the stranger who stands on the corner of Fourth and Main, holding a cardboard sign. Whether we invite him to or not, this stranger comes knocking, asking to be heard, begging to be seen. So, what to do?

Be smart, our instincts tell us. *Your spare change will not help the addict who's only going to use those dollars to get another high, another drink. Better to send a check to the local homeless shelter. Maybe vote for someone who'll mend our tattered social safety net. Besides, you can't stop for everyone. Best to keep on going.*

If you're honest—if you've ever stopped to have the conversation because your kid said, "Help him, Dad"—you know there's more to this than smarts, more than a simple, rational response. That knot in your gut that makes you feel stuck—that sounds the alarm to say, *Get out of here*—is a weight you've felt before. You felt it every time you saw the bully on the playground in elementary school. You felt it when the doctor said, "I'm sorry. It's cancer." You felt it that time when you looked out over the kids playing in the swimming pool and couldn't for the life of you spot your kid. That feeling, you know, is fear.

"Welcome everything," Rumi wrote, because however

frightening, however unwanted, the person who comes across our paths—the unexpected visitor—may be "a guide from beyond." To leave the door locked—to close ourselves off from another person in fear—is to reduce our capacity to connect, to love, to be fully human. If, indeed, this being human is a guest house, then hope comes to us, as Mother Teresa often said, in the "distressing disguise of the poor."

I am an eyewitness to all of this. But still I stop in my tracks at midnight, as I get a drink of water. I am tired from the day's work and a host of concerns. I am worried about my sick kid. Yes, that could be Jesus out on the porch, knocking. But it also could be Greg, drunk off his tail, ready to tell me (way too loudly) about how he lost his cell phone for the fourth time this month. It could be Larry, nervous as a cornered cat, wondering if I'll buy the brand-new toaster he just "found"—still in the box. Or it could be Patrice, out of her head again, wondering if she can sit and chill for a minute so she doesn't go home and "kill that big mouth, Lamont."

Over the years, I have seen a few folks get up from the dead. But I also have stared death in its ugly face, wondering if I would survive. Welcome everything, and you'll witness miracles. Welcome everything, and life can get complicated. So, as much as I cling to Rumi's wisdom and Jesus's identity as a Stranger, I also appreciate the succinct honesty of William Stafford's poem "Easter Morning." Stafford knew the miracle that can happen when you open the door and welcome a gift from beyond. "You just shiver alive," he wrote, "and are left standing / there suddenly brought to account: saved." But Stafford also knew that sometimes the stranger who comes knocking wants to sell you the moon. Sometimes the slick voice at your door will try to sell you hell, "which is what you're getting by listening." I've been there too.

So, what to do? A decade of stories flash across my mind as I stand in our kitchen, silent, half praying that whoever is outside on the porch won't knock again.

But they do.

Knock, knock.

Stafford wrote, "I'd say always go to the door, yes, but keep the screen locked. Then, / while you hold the Bible in one hand, lean forward / and say carefully, 'Jesus?'"

Is this Jesus at the door, a guide from beyond come to save me, however inconvenient his timing may be? Or is it just the beginning of another long night in the ER?

I decide to see who's there. I go for the same reason I came here to Walltown on the west side of Durham—for the same reason I've stayed. Because strangers and friends keep teaching me about realities that I'd often rather ignore. They keep inviting me to share their pain—to enter into their suffering, even. And there, in the damp, cold darkness, I learn to face myself.

I go to the door because I don't know who I am without this community of the down-and-out who have trusted me when they had every reason not to. I go to see who's there because the Jesus I want to know is the Jesus who comes knocking at midnight, bringing his tired and homeless friends with him.

Strangers at My Door is a book about the friends I've met over a decade of shared life in a house of hospitality. I wrote it because I believe these stories should be told. My aim is to hear the knock and to ask, "Who's there?" in the most immediate sense.

When we answer the knock at the door, we begin to answer the question "Who are the homeless?" In the wealthiest society to ever exist, hundreds of thousands of people live without the necessities, without a place where they belong. Homelessness has been explored as both a social problem and an issue in public-policy debates. But most of us have failed to seriously consider homelessness for what it is: the social cancer of an advanced capitalism in which people are reduced to autonomous individuals. The homeless, it may well be, are all of us, exposed.

My experience has been that we cannot face the reality of our homeless neighbors without also confronting the darkest fears and twisted desires within ourselves. So I wrote this book also as a confession of sorts. I am a "red-letter Christian" who has tried to take the words of Jesus seriously (his words were printed in red in the King James Version of the Bible that I grew up reading). While I'm not trying to make a case for Christianity and I don't assume that you buy its claims (though you very well might), I believe this stuff. I see the world through Jesus-colored glasses.

But often I have found myself sorely disappointed, both by my own easy answers and by my fellow Christians, as I've tried to wrestle with the unspeakable reality that so many homeless friends face. This book is a confession that, at precisely the places where we should have been, people of faith have often been absent. What's more, many homeless friends who have struggled in the darkness, lonely and losing hope, have prayed, "Who's there?" only to hear silence. These stories seek to honor their struggle with faith.

But this collection of stories also is an invitation to hope. Because, for all the messiness of our life at Rutba House—for all my own shortcomings, for all of our doubts and disappointments—I've leaned into the darkness, my face pressed against the screen, and I've seen the Jesus who's there—the Jesus who invites us to become a new kind of human community here and now.

This is a book about the hope that's possible when we trust a grace that's greater than ourselves and go to the door to see who's there.

Part I

Opening the Door

One

Trust

On the Bible's telling, the beginning of our human story—
the ground of our being—is a wholeness that is rooted in a reality beyond us. We did not make ourselves. We were spoken into
existence by a Voice that simply said, "Let it be."

Still, we don't get far into the story before things fall apart.
A lie is told. A brother gets killed. A building project comes undone. Follow these fractures back to their source and you find
broken relationships, a lack of trust. We are made to be at home
with our Creator, with our neighbors, with the fruit trees in the
garden. But we are homeless, this story seems to say, because a
basic trust has been broken. We push away from others, turn in
on ourselves, and so refuse the radical hospitality of creation.

Adam and Eve are exiled from the love of the home they
were made for—cut off, somehow, from the gift of simply
trusting each other. Cain is cursed to wander the earth with a
price on his head, his guard always up. We cover ourselves, each

of us, with clothes, with makeup, with advanced degrees, with home-security systems. We know we are vulnerable from the start. To really encounter someone—or to know ourselves, even—is a gift that's often beyond our imagining.

When Leah and I move to Walltown, white outsiders in an African American community, she takes a job as director of the only after-school program in the neighborhood. It seems like a good way to get to know the neighbors (through their kids, whose defenses often are not as sophisticated). The program is housed in an old elementary school building that a church now owns and operates. Leah has forty kids in a fellowship hall for three hours a day. Her job is to feed them, try to get them to do their homework, and keep them from killing one another. That last task is not always so easy. One afternoon I lay all two hundred pounds of my six-and-one-half-foot frame on a twelve-year-old kid until he agrees to let go of the butcher knife he's clutching.

The entrance to the room where Leah attempts to manage chaos five afternoons a week is directly across from a corner where a few guys in their midtwenties, dressed in long white T-shirts, stand eight to ten hours a day. (Some are cursed to wander the earth; others just stand around.) These guys greet passersby at car windows, making quick exchanges while looking over their shoulders. Leah and I talk about how we might get to know these young men from the neighborhood. We are strangers to them, and they to us, but we're about the same age.

As we go in and out the church door, the guys on the corner seem to glare. We learn that one of them is named Quinton. We find out his name because he comes into the church to use the phone. The people who work there regularly seem to know him. He doesn't bother to introduce himself to us, but Leah tries to make small talk. To connect in some way. To leap over the wall between us and this group that stands on the corner.

"So how come you so stuck up?" Quinton says to Leah one day.

"What do you mean?" she asks.

"I mean, how come y'all always passin' us out on the corner and never stop to say, 'What's up?'"

"Well, I didn't know y'all wanted to talk," Leah says. She's dumbstruck by the confrontation and isn't sure how to ask the question that's on her mind. Why does this guy who sells drugs on the corner think he can walk into a church that is filled with kids and use the phone to arrange his deals? Leah and the phone user stare at each other, two strangers with a brick wall between them.

Years later, after Quinton has decided to stop selling drugs—after he has eaten a couple hundred meals with us and has lived in one of the hospitality houses—we will laugh about all this. We will be together, telling the story over and again to soothe the pain, maybe even to begin to heal.

"Man, things was crazy back then." That is how Quinton will characterize those early encounters at the church. What he means is "I trust you now," which changes everything. Because none of us is Superman, leaping over the walls that stand between us in a single bound.

This opening ourselves to one another takes time. But love is a prisoner who stays up night after night with a sharpened toothbrush, working away at a crack in the wall until, finally, he breaks through. A way opens, not over the wall but *through* it. It helps, of course, to have someone working from the other side—someone who will meet you in the middle. But wherever the encounter takes place, this opening in the wall of suspicion and fear finally makes a relationship possible.

This opening, you learn, is called trust.

———

We move to Durham's Walltown neighborhood, strangers with white faces, because we know something about the invisible walls that partition southern towns. I was raised here—not in this city, but ninety miles away. I grew up in a town that doesn't smell as much like the New South. Driving into Durham from my hometown, we see the welcome sign on the highway that says this city was established in 1869. That's postbellum in southern history—after the war that ripped this land wide open, exposing the hidden wound of our nation's original sin. On I-85 there is a sign for Bennett Place, the farmhouse where generals met to negotiate the surrender of Southern forces in 1865. Durham is built on the fault line of America's tumultuous racial history.

George Wall was one of many freed slaves who found his way to Durham. Before the Civil War he had worked tobacco fields in central North Carolina, but as a freeman he did janitorial work for a Methodist school, Trinity College. When the school decided to move to Durham, he came with it, cutting a road through the woods north of campus to build a home for his family. A community grew up around Wall—a tightly knit extended family of other black folks, most of whom did service work on campus. The school would come to be named Duke University in recognition of the tobacco tycoon James B. Duke's financial contributions. But it would always be called "the plantation" by descendants of George Wall, who dubbed their own community Walltown.

When we move to the neighborhood, we learn there is a storefront on Knox Street called Walltown Neighborhood Ministries. It's an office that's open nine to five, with a receptionist by the door and a steady stream of people coming in and out. Between answering phones and watching the door, the receptionist greets us and makes small talk. We learn that, on the side, she designs programs for funeral services. She hands us a sample and invites us to meet Reverend Hayes, the director of the ministry.

After hearing the schedule of food-bank days, neighborhood block parties, community safety meetings, and home-ownership seminars, we introduce our idea of opening a hospitality house. We tell Reverend Hayes about the Good Samaritans in Rutba, Iraq. We pitch our vision in a two-minute elevator speech. I realize as I'm talking that this is the first person from Walltown to hear our idea. She cocks her head to the side, her eyes quizzical.

"You mean you want somebody that ain't got no place to stay to come live with you?" she asks. We see she gets the point—and that she's never heard anything like this before. Reverend Hayes starts to laugh. "Okay, when you want to start? I can introduce you to somebody right now."

She does. One block down the street and another block over, Reverend Hayes knocks on the door of a duplex. After some time, a short, dark-skinned man named Ronnie answers the door, smiles at the reverend, and invites us in. These duplexes are called shotgun houses because the three or four rooms on each side are lined up in a row, a doorway in the middle of each room. If all the doors were open, you could stand at the house's front door and shoot clear through to the back. In this duplex, all of Ronnie's belongings are boxed up and sitting in a corner. Otherwise the place is empty.

It's a friend's place, Ronnie tells us, and he had been sleeping on a couch in the front room. But his friend was evicted, and she moved all the furniture out. She doesn't know he's still staying here. Neither does the landlord, apparently. This, Ronnie explains, is why he was slow to answer the door.

We give our elevator speech about the ministry of hospitality that we hope will characterize Rutba House. It's the second time someone from the neighborhood has heard it, and I find myself choosing my words carefully. The same quizzical, disbelieving look crosses Ronnie's face as he listens to our story, but he does not laugh. Because this is not a story about someone else. It's a story he can be part of, and it's a place to sleep tonight. Ronnie starts nodding yes to every question, and we carry his belongings to our car.

In so many ways, Ronnie is the ideal guest. He's conscientious about cleaning up after himself. He helps with household chores. And in the first few weeks, he lands a job, having worn a borrowed pair of shoes to the interview. Ronnie is all smiles, and we are too. This being a guest house feels like pure gift.

Then one weekend Leah and I go out of town with Isaac, the only other member of Rutba House in those early days. Ronnie stays behind because he has to work. We make sure there's food in the refrigerator and leave the number where we'll be. Ronnie is all smiles, waving good-bye as we drive away in Isaac's car. He is our brother. We trust him.

When we return, Ronnie reports on his weekend. It was work and sleep, mostly—no time for much else. Ronnie says we're a blessing.

But on Monday morning, when Leah gets in our car to drive to work, she can smell cigarette smoke. *Odd,* she thinks, *neither of us smokes.* She can't reach the clutch so she has to adjust the driver's seat. She turns the key and then has to turn the music down. It's blaring a song she doesn't know from a CD she's never seen before.

We talk this over later and then bring it up with Isaac when Ronnie is away at work. We feel awful—like we've been lied to, like these months of life together with Ronnie have all been fake. Maybe we should give him the benefit of the doubt. Maybe he just assumed we'd be fine with him borrowing the car. Part of the work of opening ourselves to one another is learning to talk honestly about how we feel.

When Ronnie returns, we sit down together, and Leah and I tell the story. Leah walks him through her Monday morning in the car, assures him we're not angry but that we need to communicate about things if we're going to share a home. I tell him it makes me feel bad that he took our car without asking. I mention that I'm allergic to cigarette smoke. But I try to emphasize that we want to reconcile, we want to be able to trust him.

Elbows resting on his knees, Ronnie hangs his head, slowly shaking it back and forth. When we're done talking, he looks up. Ronnie's smile is gone. "I know everything looks like I took your car," he says. "But all I can say is I didn't. I couldn't stand to live with people if I did something like that."

His words prove to be prophetic. After work the next day, he doesn't come home. A couple of days later, we call his girl-friend's house to make sure he's okay. "Oh yeah, I'm fine, I'm fine," Ronnie tells us. He says he'll be home later, but we don't see him at all that week. He comes by to pick up his stuff one afternoon when we're out of the house.

A couple of months later, Leah is driving down a street just a few blocks from the house when she sees Ronnie walking the other direction. She blows the horn and waves, hoping to get his attention. He looks but doesn't seem to recognize the car. He keeps walking—all smiles—and we never see him again.

———

When I was growing up, if my momma didn't trust something that my brother or I said, she'd ask, "Can you look me in the eye and tell me that?" If we couldn't, we'd just drop it. Momma seemed to know, somehow, when the fabric of truth that held our world together was being stretched. My older brother taught me early on that there was no sense lying to her. If you weren't going to do what she said, he figured it was best to go ahead and say so. Disagreement could be negotiated, but dishonesty never paid.

At Rutba House, after being lied to a dozen times by folks like Ronnie—people with whom I've shared a bathroom—I realize that the frankness of the home I grew up in was based on a basic trust. My momma didn't have a superpower. She simply knew her boys, loving us and paying attention to our every need. Beginning in the womb, I suspect, we learned that we were loved, that someone would always take care of us, that there would be enough, that we could trust the universe. But this isn't the case for everyone. It certainly wasn't for Ronnie.

In his landmark study *The Homeless,* social analyst Christopher Jencks looks carefully at the explanations that were offered in the 1980s for the growing numbers of people who were living on the streets of urban America. "Those who end up on the streets have typically had all the disadvantages," he writes, suggesting that a guy like Ronnie isn't just down on his luck. "Most started life in families with a multitude of problems; indeed, many came from families so troubled that they [the now-homeless persons] were placed in foster care. Many had serious health and learning problems. A large group grew up in dreadful neighborhoods and attended mediocre schools. After that, most had their share of bad luck in the labor market, the marriage market, or both. It is the cumulative effect of these disadvantages...that has left them on the streets." Ronnie's experience never taught him a basic trust. Lying was the habit he learned in order to get by in a world that has no place for him.

This realization does not make it any easier to be lied to. It does not lend clarity on what to do when you're not sure which parts of a story you can believe. You wish you could be like your momma. You wish you could go back and love each person from the start, teaching them to trust, asking them—when they are tempted to spin a story in their favor—"Can you look me in the eye and say that?" But you can't. Because time hasn't healed the wounds of history, and the truth is you can't either.

The mistrust between a black man and a young white couple in a place like Walltown is personal, but it isn't private. It is written in hundreds of years of American history, before and after a war that was fought to determine whether a man like me could own a man like Ronnie.

Yes, it feels awful to be lied to. But you begin to realize that it must feel awful to be Ronnie too—awful in a way that no living-room listening session is ever going to fix. And you imagine, for a moment, the fears that must have stirred in Ronnie's soul when he peeked through the blinds of that empty shotgun house and saw you standing at the door, your white face out of place in his neighborhood. You realize you were the one who came knocking, Ronnie the one who trusted Reverend Hayes enough to open the door, to grab his few belongings, to get into your car, to be your guest when all you really had to offer was a crazy story about some Iraqis saving your friends in the middle of a war.

After you've been at this for a while, people will sometimes ask whether you're afraid, considering that you insist on welcoming strangers into your home. Eventually you realize that it's people like Ronnie who have every reason to be afraid. It is the stranger who offers you their trust when they come knocking at the door.

And you have the chance to open the door, welcoming a world that you know will change you.

When we meet Gary, he is seventeen, his uniform the baggy jeans and long white tee that all the guys on the corner wear. His is another face in the crowd of those who glare when we pass by. All they know is what they see: we are not customers, and our skin is white. All we know, personally, about the group is that Quinton thinks we're stuck up because we don't stop to talk. Between us stands a wall of misunderstanding, suspicion, and fear. From across that wall, we meet Gary.

His brother, Ant, is younger by one year. Ant is in the Walltown Neighborhood Ministries summer camp where I work for a few months as a counselor. He's a sharp kid, eager to talk, and obviously very much on his own. "Emancipated," he likes to say. He leaves camp early to go to work with a catering company and starts stopping by our house in the evenings to sit around and talk.

We learn that it's Ant's sixteenth birthday and that his favorite ice cream is chocolate, so we ask him to come by that evening after work. We'll have a little celebration. When camp is over that day, I run by Ben & Jerry's to get a tub of the best chocolate ice cream I know. By the time I get home, Ant is already there. With him, sitting on the couch, is Gary—not standing on the corner glaring at us but here in our living room, joking around with his brother. Ant has vouched for us. He's told Gary, "Listen, they're all right." Gary has walked through our door not because he trusts us but because he trusts his brother.

Later that summer, when Ant comes by after work with a terrible pain in his side, we take him to the hospital where a doctor performs an emergency appendectomy. We meet the aunt who is his legal guardian, and she tells us about the three jobs she's working and about her son who's getting out of prison. Tomorrow. She has to leave first thing in the morning to drive across the state to pick him up. We offer to take Ant to our house to recover from surgery. He ends up staying—not just until he's better but until he graduates high school, until he's done with four years of college, until he lands his first full-time job and gets his own place.

Through Ant we learn the family history—how when he was five and Gary was six, their father killed their mother and dumped her body in a field. We listen to horror stories of abusive foster families, of orphanages where Gary fought to protect Ant from other kids, of fragile times with extended family who struggled to make ends meet. We learn the story of two brothers who have, indeed, had all the disadvantages. Gary seems cursed to wander the earth, not for killing his brother but for trying to protect him. He has learned to be a fighter, his defenses always up.

Every weeknight we have a dinner for folks staying at Rutba House and any neighbors who want to stop by. Every once in a while Gary comes. He doesn't talk much, especially in groups, but we start to get to know him on his terms—the particular foods he likes, his peculiar sense of humor. We make pineapple upside-down cake for his birthday because it's his favorite, because we want him to know that we care enough to notice. He smiles a sneaky smile and says, "That's *almost* good."

Still, Gary keeps his distance. When we try to talk to him about finishing school or trying to get a job, he changes the subject. Gary is his own man, doing things his own way. He gets picked up by the police on a drug charge, and we visit him in jail. We write letters; we call his name at morning prayer. When he gets out, we introduce him to a friend who runs a construction crew, and he goes to work on a demolition job.

But three days into it, Gary quits. Our friend, he says, is racist to the core.

We start to notice a pattern—a rhythm that's repeated by dozens of guests and friends from the street. These are people for whom relationships are difficult, people who've been disappointed more times than they can count. Having been rejected, repeatedly, on the dance floor of life, they greet an open door or an extended hand with suspicion. They are desperate to connect. They long to embrace. They have fantastic, romantic illusions about the wild fun that everyone else must be having. But how can you trust an invitation to come join the supposed whirl of the rest of the world when everything you've experienced suggests there is no place there for you? What if the white guy standing there with his hand extended, holding a pineapple upside-down cake, is just one more person who's going to let you down?

Can you really trust them? The question lingers as you swallow that last syrupy bite. The pineapple upside-down cake is, you say, *almost* good.

But what if you're on the other side? What if you're the white guy who's been told in a thousand ways that gangsters who stand on the corner in white tees are a threat to your children, a plague on your neighborhood, a menace to society? What if, even though you don't want to believe it—even though you left work early to bake a birthday cake for a young man who wears the white T-shirt—you're still suspicious? What if you find yourself worrying that guys who carry drugs in their underwear and guns in their belts might do something stupid, in your house, around your friends and family, if something unexpected arouses *their* suspicion? You worry because such a thing is not outside the realm of probability. You worry because the people sitting around the dinner table are the people you love most. You worry because you are not in control, but you do everything in your power not to let it show.

One evening at dinner, a couple dozen of us are passing plates of potatoes and greens when the back door opens without a knock. Gary walks in with his friend Slug and slouches down in a chair, extra chill, asking what's for dinner. Only this time he asks extra slow, his eyelids almost closing before he can finish the sentence. We have a rule at Rutba House: anyone is welcome most any time, but no drugs and no guns allowed. You don't come to dinner high. Everyone knows this. I tell Gary and Slug that I need to talk to them in the living room, that I'm not kidding, that they need to get up. Now.

My blood pressure is up, and I say more than I need to, more than either of them cares to hear. I'm not just naming a boundary; I'm wielding words like a sword, rallying the troops to defend the castle. Gary and Slug want nothing of it. They storm out the front door, cussing my "cracker ass," insisting that I'm making a big deal out of nothing. I've only confirmed what they already knew: You can't trust white folks. They'll turn on you.

For months afterward, Gary refuses to speak to me. Eventually he starts coming around again. I apologize for being too harsh that night. We are engaged in the dance that has become so familiar. Come close, push away. Come close, push away. We're trying to learn to trust each other.

Then one spring morning, after Gary has been in prison for a year, after he's tried to make his life work in New York only to come back to Walltown, we get a call from a neighbor. Gary was shot last night, just five blocks up the street. We find him at the hospital in the ICU, a gunshot wound to the throat. He is breathing through a tracheotomy, unable to move or speak. He can open his eyes enough to glare, enough to show anyone who walks into the room that he is angry.

Gary survives, but he is paralyzed. He is a "high-functioning quadriplegic," the doctors tell us. He may regain some use of his arms, but he cannot sit up, stand, or walk. He's not likely to ever live independently. He'll have to trust someone else to take care of his basic bodily needs. He presses a button in the ICU to ask a nurse to come and suction the saliva he can't swallow.

All of this is too much for Gary. He is alive, but he is living in a rage. When he regains the ability to speak, the doctors and nurses who attempt to care for him are appalled by the way he talks to them. They call in social workers, ask for help from the psych department. We get word that the hospital administration is discussing his case as one of the most difficult they've ever handled.

Meanwhile, at our neighborhood association meeting, a lieutenant from the local police district reports on crime in the neighborhood, assuring neighbors that many of our problems have been resolved because one of Walltown's most notorious criminals has been shot. He is paralyzed, the officer has heard. The criminal won't be causing trouble on our streets anymore.

Gary continues to cause problems at the hospital. Finally, one of the medical staff calls the police. An officer arrests Gary in his hospital bed, transports him downtown, and wheels him before a judge. Then he is driven thirty miles away to the state prison hospital. His court-appointed lawyer does not return our calls. We cannot get the prison to approve a visit. We write letters, but Gary can't write back.

Four months later, when Gary finally has a court date, the prison chooses not to transport him back to Durham. A judge drops the charges, but it is not clear what will happen next. A few days later the county social services department invites us to an emergency meeting. They have received a call from the prison saying that Gary is being handed over to their care. We go downtown to sit around a table with sixteen professionals, all of whom are trying to figure out how this ever happened and what they can do about it.

Gary is delivered by ambulance to a sister's apartment, and we see him for the first time in months. He is smiling, his voice stronger now. "I'm just happy to be alive," he says. "I watched them wheel a lot of people out of there cold."

A doctor comes to evaluate Gary. She removes bandages from his feet, which unleashes the odor of rotting flesh. Dead skin hangs from Gary's heels like the limp stems of a tomato vine at the end of long, hot summer. These are pressure wounds, the doctor says, the result of flesh lying under the dead weight of Gary's paralyzed legs. He should have been turned every four to six hours. She looks over some paperwork and asks us to help roll him over to see the wound at the base of his back. The hole is so large I could put my fist in it. "This is a disgrace," the doctor says, shaking her head.

It takes a little while, but the doctor gets Gary into a rehab program at a hospital in a nearby town. They put him on a pressure-relieving bed, begin treating his wounds in earnest, and start to get him off his back for the first time in eight months. The physical therapists are amazed by his progress. They say he has advanced more in a month than many people do in years of therapy. They start to talk to him about going home, but Gary doesn't have a home. The sister, whose overdue rent has been paid by social services, is nowhere to be found. Gary asks if he could come home to Rutba House.

"I know y'all gonna have to have one of your meetings to

talk about it," he says. We do. His physical needs present a set of daunting challenges: we would have to rearrange one of our houses, build a handicap-accessible ramp, take shifts to make sure someone is always home. Logistically complicated, but doable.

The bigger challenges, it seems, are relational. Someone in our neighborhood tried to kill Gary. Can he be safe in our home? Can we? We decide we cannot know, that this is a risk love may compel us to take.

But what about Gary's relationship with us? We now have eight years of this complicated dance to reflect on—drawing near, pushing away; seeing him come close, then watching him leave. Can we trust one another enough to take this step? This isn't stopping by for dinner. He can't walk away, and we can't very well either.

After we have said yes, Leah goes to a meeting with social workers at the hospital. They sit with file folders open, reading the story in case notes and incident reports. As they talk about details, the tension grows. Leah feels like these women cannot imagine a future for Gary. They feel that she is naive. They push; Leah pushes back. Finally, one of them speaks for the group, stating their skepticism. "Do you have any idea what you are doing?"

"No," Leah says, and the social worker throws her hands up, as if to say that's what she's been thinking. "Finally," the social worker seems to say, as if she can now move forward with the task of locating a nursing home to put Gary in.

But Leah is not finished. "Of course we don't know what we're doing. But neither did I know what I was doing when I had a baby. We got help from midwives who knew more than we did. We leaned on friends and family. We figured it out as we went. I don't think we ever know what we're doing in situations like this."

No, we don't know what we're doing. As far as we can tell, this being a guest house—this experiment in welcoming everyone no matter what, in meeting Jesus in the stranger—makes you an expert at nothing. But the not knowing is itself a gift. It is an invitation, even.

When you cannot know for sure, you learn to trust. And trust, it turns out, is its own way of being in the world.

Two

Companionship

———

It's Christmas in Walltown, and we have been singing "O Come, O Come, Emmanuel" for nearly a month. In the rhythms of the ancient church that come down to us through the offices of morning prayer, we wait with captive Israel for the coming Messiah. We join our expectation with the hopes and fears of all the years.

Advent focuses our longing. "For unto us a child is born... and they shall call his name Emmanuel." God promises to come and live among us, to take up residence right here in Walltown. But for two thousand years he has been greeted in songs and Christmas pageants by shepherds who come in from the fields to find their longed-for hope lying in a cattle trough. This story invites us to keep our eyes open for gifts in unexpected guise. When a knock comes at the door, we're reminded to pay attention.

One Advent, when Leah is pregnant with our daughter, we are especially busy making preparations. Our new little person is due to arrive just after the New Year, and we want to give her a special welcome. We send her brother to stay with my parents for a weekend so we can paint the room our children will share. I get up early every morning for a few weeks, trying to finish work projects. Added to my work load is the task of assigning work to others before the baby arrives. I don't want to admit it, but I'm worried I won't get everything done.

At the end of a long week, I'm working on my laptop in the university library, just a few blocks up the hill from our house. I'm editing a set of prayers so I can send them off to other communities like Rutba House, to be used in the coming months. I jog down the marble stairs to grab some pages from the library's printer, then walk back up, proofreading on the go. I slide into the spot where I've been working, alone in the reading room.

But my computer is not on the table. Papers are still strewn about where I left them, and my coffee mug is sitting where it should be. The bag that I carry my computer in is sitting on the floor. Confused, I check to make sure the laptop is not in its bag. It's not there. I'm doing everything I can to put off admitting what I know in my gut is true. It has happened to me— and on what might well be the worst possible day.

I go down the stairs again, much more slowly this time, scanning the library for any possible evidence as to who might have taken my computer. The place is nearly empty, the halls all quiet. In the reading room I find Pervis, one of my neighbors who has cleaned this building for nearly thirty years. He's looking at a copy of the *New York Times,* listening to the clock tick slowly toward quitting time.

Pervis flashes his typical smile, but he can tell something's wrong. I tell him, and he just shakes his head. He's seen worse—far worse—I know. Pervis knows something about suffering—how it happens to all of us, how it cannot be answered, how it's best met with simple presence. He sits with me while I try to take it all in, while I shift gears from going home with the good news that my work is done and I'm now ready for the baby to come. I don't know what to say, but I know I am not alone.

At home for the past month, Leah has been struggling with gestational hypertension. The midwife says we've got to do all we can to keep her blood pressure down. She's been resting as much as is possible for a woman who does three things at once while thinking about seven other things. The community in and around Rutba House has mobilized to ease the burden of her normal responsibilities. Still, her blood pressure remains on the edge at every checkup.

I break the news as gently as I can, but Leah knows what it means. She knows that computer has the master files for a project I've been working on with dozens of people for most of the past two years. She knows it has the accounting files for the nonprofit I run, the books that track the finances that keep six people paid. She knows without asking that I'm bad at backing things up, that I probably lost a few weeks' worth of work when I was already running behind. She knows all of this and cannot put it out of her mind. Her blood pressure goes through the roof. The midwife says Leah has two choices: complete bed rest or the hospital.

We cancel our plans for holiday parties, for trips to see family, for Christmas services at church. I move a recliner into our kitchen, and Leah comes down from our bedroom once a day to keep from going crazy, to know she's not alone. We are, in the strictest sense, home for the holidays.

But as Christmas Eve rolls around and the radio stations play nothing but holiday tunes, a knock comes at the door. It's Azmen, a young woman who stayed with us for a few months a couple of years back. We haven't heard from her in a while, but she was thinking about us and decided to stop by. Then another knock. It's Quinton. "Y'all know I got to see my family at Christmas." He makes himself at home, and we tell stories and laugh about the stupid things you do when you're learning to live with strangers.

Eventually, our visitors have to go. As I walk them to the door, I see Greg coming up the block—a homeless man who is no stranger to the streets. He's smiling and hollering, "Merry Christmas," even as he stops to greet Azmen and Quinton on the sidewalk. I start to feel like I'm at a family reunion.

This goes on for three or four days. Seemingly everyone we've shared life with decides to stop by. I cook some of our favorite holiday dishes and leave them covered on the stove. Around midday I make a pot of tea. Leah remains supine in the recliner, doing all she can to keep her promise to do nothing while enjoying the company of friends. We are enveloped in a cloud of witnesses who do not sing out like a heavenly host, but they shower us with hugs and stories nonetheless.

A baby is born in Bethlehem; here in Walltown, another is on the way. At our next checkup, the midwife says Leah's blood pressure is down and the baby is doing fine. With Leah limited in her activities, she and I have more than the usual amount of time to talk. Never before have we caught up with so many former guests and friends from the neighborhood in such a short span of time. Stay home for Christmas, we learn, and most everyone shows up.

Even God, I guess. But not like a flash of light, ripping open the heavens to come down. Not like a hallelujah chorus. No, more like a baby in a manger. More like a friend sitting with you as you take in some bad news. More like a room full of folks, some who used to be homeless and some who still are, now telling stories about how they became a family.

A hospitality house reads Scripture selectively, I suppose. "I was a stranger and you welcomed me" is the quote from Jesus that we put on our doorpost. But that's not all he said. "I was hungry and you gave me something to eat, I was thirsty and you gave me something to drink." If you go back to Matthew's gospel and examine the text, these lines precede the bit about welcoming Christ in the stranger. On most any hierarchy of human needs, food and drink, hunger and thirst, are basic.

Early on in our experiment with Rutba House, Sarah starts joining us for dinner. The first time it's by invitation. She shows up dressed for a dinner party, bringing us a housewarming gift. A daughter of the South, her mother has raised her well. But ours is not the hospitality she's used to. Still, Sarah is a quick study. She keeps showing up but starts wearing a T-shirt and jeans. No gift in tow. She becomes part of the family that eats around this table.

Sarah doesn't just come to meals; she also stays after to wash dishes, to help plan neighborhood activities, to pray with our community. After several months, she asks to have a serious conversation.

All her life, Sarah tells us, she's been trying to follow Jesus—trying to take his teachings seriously, just like her mother said she should. But lately she's been experiencing something of a crisis. Jesus said, "Give to everyone who asks," but she's not sure what to do when a homeless guy on Ninth Street stops her to ask for money.

"I can give him a little money," she says, "but I know he needs more than that. I could invite him to come home with me, but that seems like a dumb move for a single woman." This is a crisis for her. Sarah is unsure how to do the thing she says she's committed her whole life to doing.

"But this hospitality house is starting to make sense to me," Sarah tells us. "I can't tell the guy on Ninth Street to come home with me. But I can invite him to come here for dinner." She does, and one evening Greg takes her up on the invitation.

Greg is a fifty-something African American man. He wears tattered construction boots, fatigue pants from an army-surplus store, and a T-shirt from the giveaway pile at Catholic Charities. The T-shirt is almost always relatively clean, not because a homeless man has anywhere to do laundry, but because the supply is bountiful enough that someone who knows what he's doing can throw away a dirty shirt and get a new one. Even still, Greg almost always smells of cheap beer.

He is, for the most part, a happy drunk. We learn that his bad days come around when he hasn't been able to get a drink by dinnertime. On those evenings he shows up for dinner sullen, or not at all. But most days he's ready to tell a story about what happened across town earlier that day, or what he found in the Dumpster behind Dollar General. Months turn into years as I listen to Greg's stories a few nights every week.

I begin to sketch a portrait in my mind of the urban scavenger's existence. A free meal at Urban Ministries, then a conversation with the guys at a bus stop. Grab some clothes between two and five on Mondays and Fridays; swing by the free food distribution downtown every other Thursday. Pick up a day of work on the labor line when you can (it's why the construction boots are a must). Every once in a while, catch a steady week of work—pennies from heaven. Thank your lucky stars, stop by the check-cashing place on Friday afternoon, and get a room at the Budget Inn. In the morning, get up late and let the water run over your head and down your back until your fingertips start to shrivel.

In the years before the late 1970s, men like Greg lived in "cage hotels" or SROs—single-room-occupancy buildings in urban centers. Such living arrangements had been common for most of a century. Following the Civil War, after hundreds of thousands of American men had been shipped off to kill other men not unlike them, an underclass of train-hopping seasonal workers emerged. They moved from harvest season in the fields to occasional factory work in cities. The "tramps" and "hobos" were more or less visible, depending on the state of America's economy and the public's willingness to embrace them.

At times, vagrancy laws were adopted to get them off the street. In other seasons, a more liberal vision of reform was promoted by social workers and aid societies. But men such as Greg never went away. In the early 1980s, after most of the nation's SROs were torn down in urban-renewal efforts, these men started showing up on street corners and in the doorways of public transit stations. Activists and government officials agreed on a name for this new class of Americans: the "homeless."

Eating dinner with Greg, I learn that his mother still lives just three blocks from Rutba House. He grew up running these neighborhood streets. One day, as he stumbles away from our house, particularly intoxicated, I stop to talk to a neighbor who's washing his car at the curb. "You wouldn't know it now," my neighbor says, "but that guy used to run like the wind." His eyes are focused on Greg.

"Oh yeah," I say. "You knew Greg when he was young?"

"Everybody knew Greg," he says, a smile crossing his face. "He ran on the track team at Hillside. Broke every record. Couldn't nobody beat him."

I hold that image of Greg alongside another in my mind. I'm watching him as he crosses an open lot on the corner of Berkeley and Knox. On this day, like others, he has had too much to drink. He catches his toe on something and falls flat on his face. I think about running to help him up but worry he'll just fall again if he is helped up. I keep cooking dinner and look out the kitchen window every once in a while to check on him.

An hour goes by. I'm pulling casseroles out of the oven, setting the table for dinner. I notice Greg is standing again in the vacant lot, his hands cupped in front of him just below his waist. He is relieving himself in broad daylight, here in the neighborhood where he is remembered as a standout, a record-setting athlete. He is doing this at the corner of two streets he used to own.

Every once in a while, Greg comes to morning prayer at Rutba House. His requests are succinct and sincere. "God, help me get something to eat today." He is translating the prayer that Jesus taught us, the one we recite every morning: "Give us this day our daily bread." Somehow, this praying for food and eating it together—this sharing of our most basic need—begins to break through the walls that separate me from Greg. I tell him stories about how I went to Washington, years ago, with dreams of ruling the world. He tells me how, when crack first came to Walltown in the 1980s, he made two thousand dollars a day and drove a different car every week. The stories around the dinner table are full of color and life, but prayer seems to cut deeper, to draw out darker tales from the recesses of Greg's soul. After prayer, when we have time to listen, Greg often wants to talk.

One morning, after we've finished singing our benediction, Greg is weeping. He tells us about the good woman he married—the woman who stood by him through prison, who promised to stay with him forever if he would just stop drinking. But he couldn't. He pounds his fist on his knee, tears streaming down his face. This is Greg's deep pain—the shame that makes everything else seem insignificant. Greg is not homeless because he was absent on the day they were handing out homes. He is poor because a thief that lives inside him has stolen everything that's precious and left him all alone. Greg's grief sits in the middle of our living room like a corpse, and there is nothing we can do. We sit shivah with him, waiting and weeping.

Of course, this does not make Greg's breath smell any better. It does not make it any less disgusting that he urinates in broad daylight within view of our kitchen window. But I am changed by the eating and the weeping together. I am changed by the invitation to share another person's grief. Greg is no longer a social problem that could be solved if we just had access to the resources. Greg is a man who shares my hunger, who wrestles with demons not unlike the ones I have learned to name in the stillness of prayer. He is a man who has been overwhelmed by the waves of suffering that are common to us all—waves that come crashing down unexpectedly, and always at the worst possible time.

I remember how, as a kid playing at the beach, I was caught off guard by a wave and thrown below the surface. Breakers roared over my head, and I knew I could not overcome this power. If the waves did not subside, I was finished. There was no purpose in fighting it, but if I waited, the water would become still again. I could then come bursting up for air. I learned the hard way that when the waters are rolling over your head, the worst thing you can do is to try to stand up.

I sit with Greg and with others as a time of singing extends into a time of silence and tears. Prayer isn't the power to stand down the waves of suffering that crash over all of us. Prayer is holding the hands of those who will stay with you, being present. It's learning to trust that a way will open. We wait for it together. Companionship is a foretaste of the fresh air we all so desperately need.

Coming up for air, we learn, often means detox. One summer night, after what feels like several weeks of holding our breath with Greg, he comes by and asks for a ride. He's ready to check himself in. The twenty-four-hour rehab center is north of town, out by the county hospital, and we make our way there. I stay until Greg is checked in, both to make sure they have room for him and to see if he's going to stay.

Driving home just after midnight, I have the windows down, letting warm, moist air wash over me. At a stop sign two blocks from our house, I hear a woman's voice. Between street-lights I can't quite make out who she is, but I wave anyway. In a neighborhood this small, you learn to be kind to everyone.

I watch the silhouette of a rail-thin woman jogging toward my car. As she gets closer, I realize I don't in fact know her, though I recognize the telltale signs of crack addiction. Her expression is cold, her tone overly serious: "I can come home with you for ten dollars." I tell her I was just waving to say hello—that I thought she was someone I knew. I tell her as kindly as I can that I wasn't seeking companionship. Then, as I look into her confused and desperate face, I ask, "Why do you feel like you need to sell yourself for ten bucks?"

"'Cause I'm hungry," she says.

"Well, I live just a couple of blocks up the street, on the right. My wife's waiting for me to get home. If you want, you can come get something to eat." I tell her the address and drive up the hill, watching my rearview mirror to see that she is following me. As I come in the door, Leah asks about Greg, but I tell her we may have another visitor soon—that it'd be best for her to talk to the woman. While I'm getting out some bread to make a sandwich, I hear a knock at the door. Leah invites the woman in. She and Leah sit down at our table, and I ask our visitor if she likes grilled cheese. She nods but doesn't say anything.

I've read in the Gospels how Jesus was a friend to prostitutes and sinners—how he ate with them and had a good time, prompting his religious critics to label him "a glutton and a drunkard." I've heard preachers describe that first-century scene, imagining the raucous laughter of people who know, maybe for the first time in their lives, that they are free.

But this is not that scene. Here at our table, late at night at a time when we're usually in bed, Leah and I are trying to make small talk with a woman we don't know. And this is just minutes after she tried to sell me her body. When she's done with her sandwich, she thanks us. She has a little food in her stomach, and maybe for a little less than the price she's used to paying. But it doesn't take the shame away. She never looks up—never looks us in the eye—just says she'd better go. We close the door behind her, climb the stairs to our room, and try to go to sleep.

Coming up for air, getting in out of the storm, grabbing a bite to eat, getting some sleep every now and then—all of these are essential for survival. But they are not, by themselves, enough to heal us. They do not, by themselves, make a home. Feeding the hungry, we learn, is not a strategy for ending hunger. And as helpful as it may be at just the right time, taking a friend to detox doesn't weed out addiction. No, welcoming the stranger is a way of getting to know people whose lives we hadn't realized were inextricably tied to ours. It is an invitation into a new family where *all* of us find a home.

―――――――

Volunteering at the monthly food bank that Walltown Neighborhood Ministries runs, we get to know Ms. Lewis. She is a late-sixties, chain-smoking, African American neighbor with a sense of humor to match her broad and sneaking smile. Everyone loves Ms. Lewis. We get used to laughing at her jokes while we stuff canned food into paper sacks.

One day, Ms. Lewis is uncharacteristically solemn. Before anyone has a chance to ask, she tells us what's on her mind. "My son's coming home from prison. He's almost forty years old—been coming home from prison since he was sixteen. I'm tired," she says. Then she looks at me and Leah. "What's that you call your house? A hospitality house? Y'all think he could live with you?"

A couple of weeks later, Ray moves in. He's a likable guy, short and bald. We can see that his inheritance is his momma's smile. Ray is accustomed to living in community—used to getting along with a bunch of other people in a small space. He's a middle-aged man who's had some success in sales, his main drawback being that his product has always been illegal. He has the gift of gab, the essential charm, a knack for connecting with people and making them like him. When he joins us, Rutba House is still a small community of four people, just beginning to process the loss of Ronnie, our first real guest. Ray becomes the life of the party.

A few weeks after Ray moves in, it's his birthday—his fortieth. We decide to pull out all the stops. "Invite everyone you know," we tell him. "We'll have a cookout in the yard." Ms. Lewis puts a lawn chair in the shade and holds court across the driveway from the grill. Cousins and friends come and go, but they're not as comfortable here as Ray and his momma are. What are they to make of this white couple and a young Hispanic man that Ray keeps calling his family? This crowd has known him most of his life. He's not getting anything over on them. They're clearly surprised—a little confused, even. Is this place good for Ray? Might this be the change he needs?

We talk a lot about what Ray needs. If we've learned anything from our few months with Ronnie, it's that hospitality isn't just throwing a birthday party. It can't be all smiles all the time. As fun loving as Ray is, we know we have to be honest about the patterns he says he wants to break out of. All around Walltown are the people, places, and things that have led him back to prison time and again.

Ray's weakness, we learn, is women. His way with words and affable demeanor make it easy to connect. It's easy to meet lonely, single women who don't mind the company of a charming, fun-loving man. But as much as they long for companionship, most of these women have little knowledge of what a healthy relationship looks like (or, for that matter, how one might start). Ray is, likewise, inexperienced in going deeper than an initial connection. At the root of all this is a fear of repeated, short-lived relationships. About the time someone really gets to know you, Ray has seen, they're done with you. Time to move on to someone else.

As we get to know Ray over several months, we come to understand why so many women are angry with him. At house meetings he is always willing to sign up for household responsibilities. Just doing his part, he says with a smile. But when his dinner night rolls around, we sometimes come to the table only to realize that Ray isn't there. He leaves no note, no explanation. When he shows up later, he offers a "Sorry, I forgot." Mostly, it's little things—dirty dishes left in the sink, forgotten commitments, missed meetings. But an accumulation of these things starts to get under your skin. Ray's irresponsible ways start to fester like a boil.

It's Leah, the only woman in the house at the time, who channels the collective anger of all the women who've had to suffer Ray's crap over the past twenty years. She decides she can't take it anymore. Ray has followed through on frying chicken for dinner, but then he leaves the pot of used cooking oil on the stove. We mention several times that it would be nice to get that pot cleaned up. Ray says, "Yeah, I'll get to it." But he doesn't.

One night when Ray is out late, doing God knows what, Leah takes the pot from the stove top, marches upstairs, and places the rancid thing in the middle of Ray's bed. If he can't deal with his own mess, she reasons, he can at least keep it in his own space.

No one is there to witness Ray's discovery of the greasy pot, but everyone on the block hears about it. Ray is livid. "I can't... I can't believe someone would do that!" He pulls the race card. "Black folk would *never* do something like that. It's just wrong."

Holding the pot in his hands, Ray is standing in the kitchen, raging. The rest of us circle up as we do every evening for prayer in the living room, next to the kitchen. We sit and listen. Everyone has a chance to speak. Ray finally puts down the dirty pan and joins us. After an hour—or maybe two— Leah has apologized and Ray has too. We end the meeting and go to bed, exhausted.

Though we cannot see it at the time, a little miracle has happened. A moment of raw honesty has exploded without everything falling apart. It is not an end, but a beginning. Ray is learning—and teaching us all—that other people can know the worst about you and still, by grace, love you. We do not have to be afraid. Leah is learning—and teaching us all—that we can tell the truth about how someone else's nonsense makes us feel and not push them away, but draw closer. We can grow into a culture of grace and truth. Together, we can know ourselves as we really are.

Of course, it doesn't happen all at once. Ray lives with us another three years, just across the hall from my and Leah's room. One time, a newspaper reporter who's writing a story about our peculiar family at Rutba House calls. She sounds concerned as she asks if I know the extent of Ray's criminal record. "I've never looked it up," I tell her, "but I understand it's pretty long." How, she asks, can we put other people in danger at Rutba House by treating Ray like he's just a normal part of our family? Do we tell other guests—do we tell people who come over for dinner—who this guy really is?

All I can say is that I don't have a quote-worthy answer to give her. Some days, I wonder about this myself.

But this being together—this knowing and being known—keeps convincing me that redemption is possible. Is it safe? No. But companionship never is. It is drawing close to another person despite our fears. It is an embrace that comes in the midst of conflict, pushing us deeper together, not further apart. It is, at its best, a glimpse of glory. But it's never safe.

When Leah and I are in the process of adopting our son, the Department of Social Services tells us they need a background check on everyone living in our household. We swallow hard. It will be difficult enough, we know, to explain the multiple misdemeanors on our collective police records. Leah and I alone account for trespassing charges incurred while committing acts of civil disobedience at the prison where our state houses its death row. We refuse to believe that anyone is beyond redemption—even those who have committed the worst crimes. So we go to the prison to remind our fellow citizens that the state is not God and does not have the power to say who is beyond hope and deserves to die.

Ray knows there's no way to explain his record. He doesn't want to stand in the way of our being able to adopt our son, so he rents an apartment behind our house. It's just twenty yards away, across the back alley.

Ray is still part of the family. He comes over to do his laundry. He joins us for dinner now and then. But he's taking more responsibility for his life now. We walk with him through another difficult relationship and have some long, good talks with the girlfriend too. This breakup doesn't end as badly. Both agree that they're not good for each other. It's a simple thing, but a breakup has never happened this way for Ray before.

When a curious visitor asks about a success story—for some "proof" that opening the door to a stranger really does make a difference—we are tempted to point to Ray. We could say that most guys like Ray are back in prison within a year. Except we've seen enough to know that the healing in Ray's life isn't the result of a well-executed strategy. It is a gift. Which isn't to say that it hasn't been a heck of a lot of hard work for Ray and for the others at Rutba House and for a dozen other people.

All that hard work has, more than anything, taught us how much we need someone like Ray to keep us honest. Grace does not come near to fix our problems, but to open our eyes to the possibility of beauty in the midst of problems.

It's Christmas again, and this year there are no crises. We host the neighborhood potluck party that has become a high point of the year. We make our favorite holiday dishes, set them out for guests to enjoy, and invite everyone to float through. Fifty, sixty, maybe seventy people show up—not all at once but in a steady, festive stream. I make the rounds, over and over, catching someone new almost every time.

In a corner of the living room, where two easy chairs angle in toward each other, I sit down to catch up with Ms. Lewis. I've not seen her for a while, so I ask about church and family— her daughter across town and her cousins in Louisiana. She has, as always, a few jokes to tell. We laugh and dip pita slices in spinach-artichoke dip.

Then, after a pause, she looks at me hard over her glasses. "You know, Ray's been in his own place four years now." I tell her I think it's been a little longer than that, even, but she reminds me that it's four years since the girlfriend moved out—four years since Ray has been paying his own bills without relying on a woman's assistance. "It's the first time in his life he's ever had his own place," she says.

Ms. Lewis's eyes are soft now, and she is smiling. "O Holy Night" is playing in the background, and I recall a line I've sung since I was a kid. "Till he appeared and the soul felt its worth." I now know clearly what those words mean. Indeed, a weary world rejoices, not because we've been relieved of our burdens but because we know we're not alone.

Dorothy Day, who started a hospitality house in New York City during the Great Depression, said it like this: "Heaven is a banquet, and life is a banquet, too, even with a crust, where there is companionship." As I sit with Ms. Lewis in a corner of the living room, pita bread is our communion. Her smile, which is for Ray as much as it is for me, is all the blessing that is needed. Our lives have been knit together, and we know it is a gift.

A soul feels its worth, and it is mine.

Three

Saved

———

In Walltown the "saved" are a class, not unlike the rich and the poor. The saved are distinguished from the unsaved by sanctified speech, rejection of strong drink, and, most importantly, devotion to the household of God. In Walltown the saved go to church, and they tend to stay there. Those counted among their number have a story to tell about how they crossed over from the realm of darkness and destruction into the city of marvelous light. These stories of social mobility are called testimonies, and they are the bread and butter of religion in this place. The saved love to talk about how bad off they used to be and how good God is.

On Wednesday nights we have a praise-and-testimony service at our neighborhood church, and that is when I tune my ear to this genre of storytelling. It begins not with "Once upon a time" but with "Giving honor to my Lord and Savior Jesus Christ." These tales offer a window into the suffering my neighbors have known. The stories often sound as desperate as a country song—and as sad and lonesome as the blues. But I know to anticipate the turning point. "Just when I thought I was lost, my dungeon shook, and the chains fell off." Jesus shows up in these stories, and folks are saved.

I'm introduced to a neighbor named Jeremiah who is known as Bike Man. He's a Walltown fixture when we move in. Jeremiah is not a storyteller, but he is a man who knows how to work with his hands. He rides a blue ten-speed everywhere he goes and fixes anything that breaks—on bikes, for sure, but also on small engines, on household appliances, on old porches with floorboards that are beginning to rot. His is a gentle spirit, always ready to listen. I enjoy chatting with him on the corner about the weather or his latest project.

I'm left to wonder about his story. He has, as far as I can tell, spent most of his life in Walltown. He knows everyone by name, and he is known. But Jeremiah is a loner. While Greg, who is of the same generation, almost always has someone with him, Jeremiah rides solo. An urban cowboy of sorts, he isn't asking anyone for anything. He's just getting by, one day at a time, keeping his chin up and his eyes fixed on the horizon.

Maybe it's because his honesty and self-reliance remind me of men I grew up around; maybe it's just happenstance. But somehow, Jeremiah and I become friends. We're not middle-class friends who get together for coffee; neither are we working-class guys who grab a beer at quitting time. We're a twenty-something white guy and a fifty-something black guy, a graduate student and a homeless man. We're two people from two different worlds whose lives just happen to have intersected. Yet we like each other. Something inside me comes to life when I see Jeremiah. We sit around and talk when we both have other things we should be doing, just because we want to, just because being together feels like a gift.

Jeremiah is a man who knows how to diagnose a problem. "My trouble," he tells me one day, "is that I can't stop drinking." I don't know his whole story, but I know some of the facts. He has a daughter whom he adores but doesn't get to see much. He has other family around, but bridges have been burned. He has some drinking buddies that he stays with sometimes, especially when it's cold. But Jeremiah is too independent to stay anywhere for long, too proud to ask someone else to feed him or put a roof over his head. His life is a bicycle that works and jobs that he picks up and is good at. People trust the work of his hands, but a gear keeps slipping. The problem is his alcoholism.

"Well, you know, you're not the only one," I tell him. I've just been to a praise-and-testimony service, and half a dozen stories remain fresh in my mind. These stories are not my story. I never had an uncle who abused me or a mother who left me. I never smoked dope with friends from the neighborhood or sold crack to try to get ahead. I've never once just wanted to get away from it all. Jeremiah knows these things. But I mention that a lot of the folks at our church tell stories about facing into the depths that he is facing. "They've learned that God meets them there," I say. "They've learned that God loves them, especially there in the darkness."

Jeremiah smiles and drops his head. "But, Jonathan, you know church ain't for me."

"Church is for everybody," I say. And I quote a line that finds its way into most testimonies: "God is no respecter of persons. Jesus loves us all the same."

"Oh, I know that," Jeremiah says, still smiling. "But church ain't for people like me. I don't look the part."

I know he's right. The saved have a dress code for Sunday mornings and a rule book for every other day of the week (when people are looking, at least). They're a generous bunch, for sure. They'll buy you a suit from the thrift store to wear when you come to walk the aisle on Sunday morning. But what if you're the sort of person who would never feel comfortable in a suit? What if you're Jeremiah, and all that whooping and hollering on Sunday morning just doesn't do it for you? What if, when you come to the end of your rope, you can trust the hand that reaches out to save you but you still don't want to live among the saved?

I do not for a minute deny the power that has changed

everything for the saints who testify about the goodness of God in the land of the living. Jeremiah doesn't either. He knows that Sunday morning is good news for the saved. He knows that it's good for me. But he also knows—and just as surely—that it's not for him. The church teaches the love of God, and at our best we embody it. But we don't own it. Sometimes people like Jeremiah know the love of God for themselves, at the point of their deepest need.

Sometimes they are Jesus to us.

And we are saved.

One morning when I'm still in grad school, before I've left for class, the phone rings. "Jonathan, I need you." It's Bobby, who is nothing if not direct. "I need you to go downtown with me. I've got to go to court."

Over the phone I can't make out exactly what the charge is, but I tell Bobby I'll stop by in the afternoon to read the paperwork with him. I find him at "home" on Sedgefield Street, just around the block from us. It's a large rooming house on the corner with its windows boarded up. Because we came here looking for a big house where we could live in community with other people and still have room for guests, this house had caught our eye. We know that its owner, a local slumlord, died about a year ago. Settling his estate became a complicated matter, and the property has been stuck in a sort of legal limbo. People in real estate know the story. Bobby does too. He's been squatting in a downstairs bedroom for several months.

Bobby gets around on a bicycle that he does not pedal but pushes uphill by shuffling from one foot to the next. He keeps the bicycle beneath him because his legs don't have the strength to hold him up. His head is a shock of white hair; his long, unkempt beard the same color, except for the deep-brown snuff stains. In a different life, he might play Santa Claus. But he looks more like John the Baptist, the wild-eyed prophet whose voice cried out in the wilderness, preparing the way of the Lord. Bobby has an untamed look, and his presence is an affront to most people.

Which is why, considering the general level of chaos on food distribution days and Bobby's physical limitations, I offer to deliver his bag of food to him. I'll be stopping by the food bank at Walltown Neighborhood Ministries, so it's no trouble. "Just let me know where to bring it," I tell him. And after looking at me real hard, he agrees. I knock on the downstairs window that he had specified, and a chorus of barking breaks out. I can tell by the pitch that small dogs are inside, so when Bobby comes to the door, I watch my ankles.

This squatter's life is sustained, I learn, by the free food I'm delivering, along with a portion of a niece's Social Security check and money that Bobby gets by sitting at the top of an exit ramp on the Durham Freeway, holding a sign that reads Homeless: Please Help. It is this third income stream—the public begging—that has gotten Bobby into trouble with the law. When I stop by on the afternoon after Bobby's morning phone call, he shows me a citation for soliciting without a permit and "failure to wear proper equipment." I too am confused. I write down the court date in my pocket planner and tell Bobby I'll pick him up that morning to go to the courthouse with him.

Before court is in session, we line up with everyone else who's there due to a speeding ticket or expired vehicle registration. An assistant from the district attorney's office stands at the front of the line asking to see paperwork, then sending people to one side of the courtroom or another. When we get to the front of the line, I note the contrast between Bobby, leaning on a walker and smelling every bit like someone who lives in an abandoned house with seven dogs, and this young prosecutor, dressed in a pinstriped suit, cleanly shaven with fresh gel in his hair. He reaches for the citation without saying anything, and Bobby launches into the speech that he's been rehearsing.

The man from the DA's office does nothing to acknowledge Bobby's presence or his words. "Why do they keep sending us these?" he mutters under his breath. Then, looking at me, he hands the paperwork back and says, "I wash my hands of this."

We're sent to another courtroom, where a judge explains to Bobby that a recent city ordinance requires anyone who is begging in public to purchase a solicitation license and, for their own safety, to wear a reflective orange vest. He directs us to the business license office in the courthouse basement, where I help Bobby fill out an application and make the ten-dollar capital investment in his newly established small business. Bobby has jumped through the hoops of a system that has no time for him. He is, for the moment, saved.

"I thank God for you," he tells me a dozen times before we can get back to his house. "I thank God for you."

I keep thinking about the DA's assistant, wondering if he realizes that he had imitated Pontius Pilate. He had treated Bobby the same way God was treated when he had his day in court two thousand years ago. "Foxes have holes, and birds of the air have nests," Jesus is reported to have said at the time, "but the Son of Man has nowhere to lay his head." In Jesus, God became not only human but also homeless. And when as a homeless Man he stood in Pontius Pilate's court, Jesus had to listen to the authorities' estimation of his worth.

Of course, the irony of the gospel story is that the homeless Man who is dismissed by Pilate is the Person who matters most in the story, the One who will save us all. But dramatic irony is little comfort to a man like Bobby, who is used to being treated like dirt.

At church we sing:

Jesus knows all about our struggles,
He will guide till the day is done;
There's not a friend like the lowly Jesus—
No, not one! No, not one!

I'm not sure if it's any comfort to Bobby that Jesus, the
God-Man, was also a homeless man like him, familiar with
suffering and rejected by the powerful. Bobby doesn't talk
about Jesus that way. By walking with Bobby, I get to know this
Jesus who is a Man of no reputation, despised by the world. I
was raised by good church people, and I've known Jesus all my
life. I went to Washington, DC, at age sixteen to work for a US
senator, to get a head start on the trickle-down approach to
changing the world for Jesus. In the name of Jesus, I wanted to
be a Pontius Pilate for the common good.

But a homeless man derailed me in front of Union Station.
I was rushing to lunch one day, and a fellow with a Styrofoam
cup asked if I could spare some change. I was in a hurry, and I
ignored him. But I heard the voice of Jesus speak to me in the
King James English that I had memorized: "Inasmuch as ye did
it not to one of the least of these, ye did it not to me." I never
learned the man's name, but he changed the direction of my
life. I can't share my testimony without talking about that

homeless man in DC. Now I am suddenly aware that he was Bobby—he was the nuisance that the system would have flushed out if it could. And I aspired to be the authority in the pinstriped suit who pulled the flush cord.

I'm uncomfortable with Bobby's thanks, reluctant to even acknowledge his suggestion that I am God's messenger sent to give him some comfort in a life that is, more or less, hell. As long as I know him, I'll always change the subject when he tries to thank me. I'll always tell Bobby that it's a gift to know him, that I'm glad for the chance to do what I can. I tell him those things until eight years later, when I call a funeral home five counties over and give them my credit card number. They will cremate Bobby's remains and mail them back to Durham.

But you don't realize until it's all over and you're writing it down how these awkward exchanges give you the only language that can begin to describe what has happened—how Bobby was, in truth, an angel to you. He was God's messenger. You don't know until the day of his memorial service how seeing the assistant DA through Bobby's eyes helped you resist your worst demons—your career goal to replace Pontius Pilate. In a moment of clarity, you see the pure joy that can erupt in the midst of struggle, even when the pain doesn't go away. And you know that it was Bobby who opened your eyes, little by little, to see how you're being saved.

"I thank God for you," you say, echoing the language that

Bobby taught you. "I thank God for you," you say over and again, realizing that he must have meant it as much as you do.

———

A hospitality house, you learn soon enough, is sustained by a grace that's beyond you—beyond your community meetings and your lofty commitments—to see the stranger as a gift. There is, for sure, always work to be done. Yet nothing you do guarantees that any of this will be here tomorrow. You think often of Clarence Jordan, the Baptist radical from south Georgia who started an interracial commune in the 1940s. After facing threats and boycotts, firebombs and bullets for two decades, Jordan reflected that his experiment was "forever dying and forever living." Every day a resurrection. This way of living leads a person to pray.

Life and people like Bobby help teach us to pray. So do Benedictine monks, who have devoted themselves to this discipline for fifteen hundred years. Prayer, for them, includes trying to welcome every visitor in the same fashion they would welcome Christ. There is no remaining romanticism that accompanies such a commitment. It is, for the Benedictines, a very human reality—a complex part of the life they've been given.

"Benedict taught us to greet every guest as if the guest were Christ," a monk says to me with an exaggerated earnestness.

And then, with a twinkle in his eye, he adds, "But sometimes, when the knock comes at the door, we say, 'Oh Christ, it's *you* again.'" He chuckles, and I know he knows how much I need the prayers he's teaching me.

Some Benedictines pray as often as seven times a day, getting up even in the middle of the night to chant psalms in an expectant vigil. Every army needs its special forces, I suppose. The highly disciplined soldiers who walk point on battlefields open paths for those who follow. In a similar way, we trust that there are others—the called, the specialists, the experts—to do the heavy lifting of prayer. At Rutba House, we settle into a rhythm of morning and evening prayer, beginning and ending the day circled up in the living room. Pictures of Martin Luther King Jr. and Dorothy Day hang on the walls to inspire us and remind us that we are not alone as we sit silently and listen.

Our rhythm of prayer and listening is fairly well established by the time that Ant, Gary's younger brother, has his bout with appendicitis. At age sixteen he comes home from the hospital to stay with us. He recovers and resumes his gregarious ways, busy with school and work and his friends on the lacrosse team. He has, by his own account, never had much of a schedule, bouncing around between foster care and extended family since he lost both parents eleven years earlier. He says he thinks he could probably use a little structure. So I explain our rhythm of praying together and eating together. I wax eloquent about the ways that prayer and dinner feed body and soul, knitting us together as a new kind of family. My Benedictine mentors would be proud. But they didn't know Ant.

"My dad killed my mom when I was five years old," he says. "I don't do religion. If there is a God, I don't like him."

Fair enough. I tell Ant I can understand his position. None of this is required; it's just something we've learned that we need. We give him our schedule of prayers and meals, tell him he's welcome any time. For two years, until he graduates from high school, Ant avoids our prayer times without exception.

But then, the next fall, when he's reading the sermons of Martin Luther King Jr. for an Intro to the African American Experience class, Ant calls home. He says, "I think I'm starting to understand why y'all do what you do." We talk about the radical love ethic of Jesus and the power of the Civil Rights movement. Ant is a student at a college in Greensboro, North Carolina. In 1960, four students from that school went to a Woolworth's store and sat at the lunch counter, waiting to be served. In the Jim Crow era, such an act was tantamount to sedition. The students' action set off tremors, launching a sit-in movement that was one of the defining developments early in the Civil Rights movement. Ant is soaking in the spirit of the college and its place in American history. And he mentions that he is telling his friends about Rutba House.

I learn that a Civil Rights veteran who has been a mentor

to me, John Perkins of Mississippi, is going to be in town. I contact the organization that is hosting his visit and offer our church as a venue for John's workshop. I call Ant and tell him I'd like him to come. "Put the date on your calendar," I say. "I'll send you a train ticket."

As John is sharing his testimony in the church fellowship hall, talking about what it was like to grow up without a father or a mother—without the "institutions of love," he says—I look over and see a tear on Ant's cheek. "On that day when I met Jesus, I knew that I was loved," John says. He goes on to recount how love spurred him to action—how he developed a whole philosophy of Christian community development out of the experience of trying to love his neighbors in the rural Mississippi community where he started working in the 1960s.

Having captivated the crowd with his story and his wit, John fast-forwards to the present. "The problem in our communities," he roars like a prophet, "is that little black boys look around and they don't see anybody who looks like them loving them." His altar call, as it were, is for young black men to commit to teach in the public schools.

Ant goes back to Greensboro and talks to his advisor about how to change his major from pre-law to education. He puts in an application to come back to Walltown the next summer as a counselor in our neighborhood summer camp. It is, he knows, a faith-based camp—a camp that invests as much time in Bible study and prayer for the counselors as it does in fun activities for the kids. "I still don't know what I think about God," Ant tells me, "but I'm starting to like Christians."

The summer after Ant graduates from college, before he goes back to school to get his master of arts in teaching, he lands his first full-time job teaching a digital-literacy curriculum to middle school and high school students at our Walltown Recreation Center. Ant recruits the kids himself—these younger brothers, cousins, and nieces of guys he grew up with. They adore Ant, and his program manager is amazed. "I saw Ant walking those kids on a field trip," this guy tells me one day. "He looked like the Pied Piper with that train of kids following him out of the neighborhood!"

I think about how few of those kids have a father at home— and how there are at least a dozen Pied Pipers in this neighborhood. But unlike Ant, the others are bitter that they haven't gotten their due, and they lead our kids away to gangs and prison and untimely deaths. These kids follow because the guys on the corner, pied in their reds and blues, look like them; they talk like them. They have known their pain.

But so has Ant. Only he also has known something more than pain—something more than the despair that comes from being abandoned. He has glimpsed the love that can come in the midst of life's worst mess. This, he knows, is the love that gave the students sitting on soda-fountain stools at

Woolworth's, back in 1960, the courage to stand their ground. They did it without striking back when angry white folks spit in their faces. But that was more than fifty years ago. What's more important, Ant knows, is that this same love is real today. It's what makes it possible for him to stay.

This Pied Piper of Walltown is not leading kids on a nihilistic march away from the world that did him wrong. He is teaching them by example—he is teaching me, I realize—what it means to walk in the way of love. On my worst days, when it feels like there's more of the dying than the living around here, I stop and think of Ant. Not every testimony gets told in the language of Wednesday evenings. But when love meets you at your lowest point, the story's true in any language.

When Jeremiah pulls up in front of the house on his bicycle, I realize I haven't seen him in weeks. Like a call from my best friend who lives hours away, Jeremiah's gentle smile, there beneath his signature baseball cap and sunglasses, slows me down and puts me at ease. I suddenly forget whatever it was I was going to do. I want to sit with him with glasses of sweet tea in the rocking chairs on the porch. But Jeremiah doesn't push his bike up the hill into our yard. He stands with it balanced between his legs, leaning forward on the handlebars, looking a bit like Bobby, only without the wild eyes and the tangled beard.

He has bad news. Jeremiah went to the hospital with a pain in his leg, and after taking an x-ray, they told him that a bone had broken, that it was weakened by cancer. The cancer, they said, is all through his body.

"I've got to go in for them to do some surgery," he says. "I guess I'll have to sober up." I tell him to call me when he gets there, to go ahead and plan to come home to our house when they'll let him. He writes our phone number on his hand, and a week later he's back at our place but this time on crutches.

We move Jeremiah into the bedroom just off the front of the house, beside the downstairs bathroom—the room that Leah and I lived in for a year until we realized that in a house like this you want to sleep as far from the center of action as possible. It is, we've learned, the best room for hosting guests who need care. Plenty of room for visitors, easy access to a bathroom, within earshot of the living space where we pray and eat and carry on. A few folks have recovered in this room, but we know that Jeremiah is coming to die.

When word gets out that the end is near, family members start showing up. Jeremiah is glad to see them, but it's clear that these relationships are complicated. He has a sister who seems to be taking charge of things for the family. She has, we learn, a life insurance policy on her baby brother. I do not doubt that she cares about him, but life has been hard for both of them and her interests are mixed. Jeremiah is worth more to her dead than alive.

When we have time to talk, between the practicalities of life and the chaos of family, Jeremiah wants to talk about God. He is in pain, I know, but he doesn't want to talk about that. His smile is tired, yet it's there just the same. "I'm thankful," he tells me. "God has been good to me." Jeremiah is not troubled by the whys that nag at so many people when they're forced to look death in the face: *Why now? Why me? Why this?* He seems, rather, to be overwhelmed by God's goodness. "I'm just glad I can be sober, glad I can be here with y'all." All of this, he seems to believe, is somehow a gift from God.

When the folks from hospice say it's time, Jeremiah goes to stay at a house they staff with twenty-four-hour nursing care. He lasts a couple of weeks more; then he is gone. The sister with the life insurance policy calls to tell us. She makes the funeral arrangements at a church across town, a place where she has some connection. We go early to the service, and there is Jeremiah, laid out in a shiny casket and dressed in a brown suit.

A preacher who didn't know Jeremiah stands and says some things about God. Most of it is true, I guess, but it rings hollow with Jeremiah lying there, not looking like himself. After the eulogy that's printed in the program has been read, there's a time for people to stand and share something. The preacher asks that the remarks be kept to three minutes. A niece, who seems about as comfortable in church as Jeremiah was, doesn't need that much time. All she has to say is this: "I never once heard my uncle tell a lie."

I think how strange a testament this is about a lifelong alcoholic—that he never lied, never tried to deceive this member of his family. I think about the time I knew Jeremiah, and I realize this niece has summed up what I loved about this man: wrestling his worst demons and struggling to get by, Jeremiah learned to tell the truth. In the end, the truth that remained was that God is good and we are loved. For Jeremiah, that was enough.

Part 2

Leaning In

Four

All of Us, Exposed

Ray is our resident expert on addiction. When he was still a kid, he learned how a substance can get its tentacles wrapped around you. He is an authority on the ways in which a high, like a god or a nation, can demand ultimate allegiance. This education landed Ray in the juvenile corrections system, where his people skills allowed him to develop a broad social network among those who go for cheap beer and crack cocaine.

The experience stood him in good stead for future business success. As an adult, Ray engaged these resources to generate an income stream. The options are limited for an ex-con, he reasoned. You've got to do what you've got to do. He became a dealer.

The ugliest part of exploitation is how, at the very bottom of society, the worst violence is committed against the disadvantaged by the disadvantaged. It's a messed-up world where a man tries to make something of himself by selling the thing that nearly destroyed him. And he does this to people he grew up with. Such moral contradictions become a breeding ground for self-deception. There are a thousand ways you learn to justify your actions. You keep fooling yourself, while at the same time you keep your guard up to make sure you're nobody else's fool. Hustling hones a particular skill set. You learn to sniff out the worst in people. You learn how to watch your back.

And even when, by some grace you don't entirely understand, you come to yourself and decide this is not who you want to be and that your only hope is to be born again from the start, you can't help but remember what you have learned about people. You can't help but look at others and see greed, self-deception, and an ingrained preference for saying whatever it takes to keep working the con. As we sit at dinner at Rutba House and talk with people who need a place to stay—many of them because their addiction has led them to homelessness—we learn that Ray is a gift. He has a keen sense for when someone is serious about recovery and when they're just gaming. We learn to trust Ray's sixth sense. If he's ready to welcome someone, they're probably ready to be real with us.

Which is why, when Ray tells us about his friend Ken who's coming home from prison, we act fast to make space for him. Ken is serious, Ray tells us. He's not messing around. Besides, he's like a brother. Ray would trust him with his life. Ken just needs a place to stay until he can get his feet on the ground. We offer him a room for a couple of months, and he moves in just before Thanksgiving.

We are an extended family of sorts—a broad community of married and single people with different work schedules and skill sets, all committed to sharing what we have and making a life together. We are not a shelter, maximizing our resources to most efficiently meet the pressing need. We are a community— a peculiar sort of family—that must maintain a delicate balance between guests and hosts, employed and unemployed, workers and visionaries, do-ers and be-ers. Growth requires not only more space but also more people who can be successfully integrated into our family system. We have our limits. But we decide one summer that we can add three single men, all of whom are in graduate school, and we rent a house across the street for them to stay in.

It's a three-bedroom place, so two of the guys double up to leave a room available for a guest. Ken is their first. We've already planned to have our Rutba House family Thanksgiving dinner around the table at the new house, and it happens that this is Ken's first night there. Everyone has made their favorite holiday dishes, and the whole extended family shows up—both the people who live in our houses and the neighbors and friends who've become part of the family.

We are thirty-some people in all, spilling out of the combined kitchen and dining area into the living room, where we sit with plates balanced on our knees. When everyone has had their fill, we get out the sparkling apple juice, pour a round for everyone, and offer toasts for all the people and experiences that we're thankful for. John, one of Ken's new housemates, raises a glass. "We're glad you're here," he says to Ken. "Welcome to our family."

The next day, because classes are out of session for the students at the new house, they're gone most of the day, enjoying holiday celebrations with friends and family. One of them invites Ken along, but he says no, he'll just enjoy the peace and quiet at home. When the guys get back, Ken is gone. Also missing are three laptop computers.

Ray is furious. He makes some calls and learns that Ken sold the computers to a guy on the corner, then bought crack with the proceeds and left the neighborhood. We tell people who might know something that we'll buy the computers back, that the semester's worth of work that's saved on them is more important to these guys than the value of the hardware. But the hard drives are already too far gone in the complex black-market web, in which people participate as anonymously as possible. Ray keeps working until he finds Ken and gets him on the phone. "Here, you talk to him," Ray says, handing me the handset. I step out onto the porch.

"Are you all right?" I ask Ken, and he says yes. "Well, I'm glad to hear it," I say. "We've spent most of the day trying to find you and the rest of it trying to help these guys get their schoolwork back." In spite of my best effort at self-control, I can hear the bitterness in my voice. However valid my anger may be, it's not going to help the situation. I decide to change my tune. "Listen, I know you're struggling with a lot and you probably feel really guilty about this, but I want you to know we forgive you. We'd like you to come back so we can talk about what you need to stay clean."

Ken says he'd like that too, that he'll come by tomorrow. But he doesn't. Maybe it's the shame, or maybe it's that crack has gotten hold of him and won't let go. Maybe he just can't trust that I mean what I said. We never see Ken again. Ray says, "I'm sorry, y'all. I thought he was ready." We tell him that we did too — that you can never know for sure. But, of course, Ray knows this too well. What's getting under his skin is the fact that addiction is a beast that won't be tamed. It lurks in the shadows, hides beneath the surface, like the prowling lion mentioned in Scripture, "seeking whom he may devour." Only this animal isn't threatening to take Ray's laptop. Every time it growls, he knows it could take his life.

***

Talk to anyone *from* Walltown, anyone who grew up here in the fifties and sixties, back when the streets weren't paved. They will tell you how crack changed the place. Walltown always had its challenges, ghettoized by racism and handicapped by poverty. But Walltown was a proud community, electing its own mayor, organizing block parties and Friday-night dances, posting a guard of men on its northern border to shoot the rats that crossed over from the city landfill.

People who grew up here in those days sat-in at lunch counters when they were still in high school, heard Dr. King when he came to town, and went off to college to learn how to make their way in business, in law, as professors, and in government. Many of them are now retired, and they organize a Walltown Reunion every Fourth of July weekend. Six hundred people come out for a Friday-night dance, a Saturday-morning parade, a carnival at the recreation center, and Sunday-morning worship at the church. In the liturgy, everyone vows to love and serve Walltown "until death do us part."

These same people will tell you how Walltown changed—how crack arrived in the eighties and they started getting calls from their mommas about the guys they saw standing on the corner and the gunshots they heard at night. These daughters and sons of Walltown did what they could: they put a security system in for momma; they told her to call the police. But they weren't here to help her negotiate the complexities of children who saw economic opportunity in the drug trade or grandkids who got hooked on the stuff. They weren't here to watch a generation go off to jail and come home marked as "criminal," caught up in a system that would inevitably take them away again.

Twenty years later, I'm sitting at the kitchen table late one night, talking to a man who's grieving because his momma has died. He spent the last years of her life either away at prison or bouncing between the shelter and the street. "They tell me crack changed Walltown," I say to him, and he has just enough alcohol in him that he wants to talk. "Man, yeah," he says. "Nobody'd ever seen that stuff over here." His hollow face brightens at the memory of that initial discovery. "I started selling the stuff, and it took off. The delivery man was bringing it to my front door, overnight from New York. I had three cars in the driveway, making two thousand dollars a day. Two thousand *a day*," he repeats, looking like he can almost feel it in his pocket. Of course, it didn't last. But how's a kid who always had to wear hand-me-downs supposed to resist an opportunity like that?

These moments of honesty tend to come in one-on-one settings, when someone's guard is down, when they're not playing their onstage role but just being themselves. Anyone who sits on their porch and pays attention can watch what goes on in our neighborhood—the exchanges that happen when guys stop to embrace one another or when a woman catches a cab late at night, dressed in sequins. But there is no public conversation about the underground economy that feeds on humanity's basest desires.

———

Leah is talking to a neighbor who works as a prostitute—a friend who's having a particularly hard time with the husband who's also her pimp. Leah feels she can ask what seems like the obvious question: "Why do you put up with this? You're a beautiful, capable woman. Why hop in a cab and give yourself to these men whenever they call?" Our neighbor is not fazed by the question. She has thought this through. "Men are simple," she says to Leah. "They only want one thing. Why not make yourself up and perform a little for the rich ones? I can make more money in one trip to the hotel than I could make in three days of waitressing at some man's restaurant. I'm beating him at his own game."

Maybe you can't tame the beast, but there is a logic that suggests you do your best to try to harness its power in a mean world where it's every woman for herself. Only this world is never that simple. It is not a world that is reducible to an economic calculus, no matter how hardened you might be. This neighbor, whose view of men has been diminished by a long succession of johns, is nevertheless in love with the husband who both uses and protects her. At his best, he has loved her for who she is. They've known better days when he had work, when he provided for their family, when he even talked about serving the Lord. But life has spiraled once again into the madness that reminds them they are not in control. They are subject to forces far stronger than either of them.

Given the terrible wounds that these two bear, Leah and I split our more intense conversations with them along gender lines. When they're willing to talk, Leah goes with the woman to a quiet place in the house. I sit down in the kitchen and listen to him. In the midst of this present crisis, he's intensely interested in finding peace. He wants to talk about prayer. I probe for some of his backstory, wondering what leads a man to rent his wife out on weeknights as an escort to businessmen. His story, it turns out, explains a lot

He was, he tells me, an accident—born to a mother who worked as a call girl in New York. He grew up in a brothel, sleeping in the corner while his mother plied her trade. When he was old enough, he was put to work cleaning up after the addicts who passed out on the couch. He learned to be careful with the needles, to negotiate the mood swings that are exaggerated by drugs. He learned to hate the stuff, but he also learned its power. By the time he was twelve, he was selling drugs on the street. By the time he was twenty, he was advancing to bigger things, learning the inner workings of a multibillion-dollar industry that operates in secret.

Sometime in his twenties, he tells me, he was approached by the corporate training program of a multinational corporation that sells carbonated sugar water. He put on a suit and went through their management school. They offered him a job, he says, but he decided that their system was worse than the one he'd been born into. Corporate America seemed little more than an airbrushed mirror image of the hell he knew he should run from. Maybe he just needed to downsize, he thought—to get out of the big city. This is how he ended up getting married and, for these few months, living on our block.

I remember a passage from Thomas Merton, the ambitious Columbia University graduate-turned-monk who became famous in the midtwentieth century for writing with powerful honesty about his struggle to find meaning in the modern world. "We live in a society," Merton wrote in 1948, "whose whole policy is to excite every nerve in the human body and keep it at the highest pitch of artificial tension, to strain every human desire to the limit and to create as many new desires and synthetic passions as possible." What Merton could see from a monastic cell, as he faced the demons that had driven him as an ambitious modern man, my neighbor has experienced in living color, played out in front of him—and performed by him and by those he loves—since before he can remember.

"The addict," a mentor says to me one day, "is all of us,

exposed." When he says it, I know what he means. Maybe we are, in the language of the psalm, created "a little lower than the angels." But I think how I always have been like Icarus, envious of the angels' wings, pushing the limits of creativity and gift to see if I might rise a little bit higher, a little closer to the sun. Twenty-three million Americans over the age of twelve—nearly 10 percent of the population—are addicted to alcohol or drugs. That's not counting the sixty-one million who get their high from nicotine, our most addictive known stimulant, nor the countless others who are hooked on sex, shopping, pornography, food, or work. If we're honest with ourselves, addiction is not an anomalous disease of the poor. Addiction is our way of life.

Trouble is, we're not honest with ourselves. The telltale sign of addiction—the thing that will tip you off time and again as you try to make a life with people in recovery—is lying. Addicts lie about things they don't need to, things that don't make any sense. Like a cartoon that exaggerates its subject's strongest feature, addiction highlights our deepest fears. We scramble to hide the tortured pleasure that is our deepest shame. But no amount of self-flagellation will fix our twisted desires. The only way to begin to heal is to open our wounds to the air and the light, to let the gentle grace of forgiveness meet us in a place where we're known and loved.

In time you see that this is why you're here, that this is what you have to learn from the guests whose problems are so much more obvious than your own. You were not born in a brothel; you've never been so low that you were tempted to think a dime bag could lift your spirits. But you've hoped and prayed just as recklessly that you could rule your little world, tackle the enemies you can see, and live to tell the story. You've mixed adrenaline with caffeine to help you finish projects, giving no thought to the sickness that will inevitably strike when you're coming down from your high of intensive work. You did not think about the people who would have to step in and care for you.

But when you are in bed, feeling sorry for yourself and a little bitter that your waxen wings melted so easily, a voice calls from outside your room. It is not your wife. She is busy taking care of the kids and a half dozen other things that you can't do today because you are lying here. It is, instead, the recovering crack addict who came to your door years ago for help.

"Can I get you anything to eat?" he asks. And you know that this is the help you need, even though you didn't know to ask for it. This is what recovery looks like: one needy person helping another see that he cannot make it on his own.

I know about Mac's addiction because we are in church together, because he is courageous enough to stand up on Wednesday night and talk not just about the goodness of the Lord but also about the demons he's fighting. I read between the lines for a few months until one evening he names his struggle: he's been using again, and he knows he needs help.

Mac has been my neighbor since we came to Walltown. I know he is the thirteenth son of sharecroppers from South Carolina—a relative newcomer, like me, to this neighborhood. He catches a bus every morning to a job on the south side of town. When he gets home in the evening, he works in the yard outside his apartment, always eager to talk about the tomatoes he's growing or the rosebush he's trying to transplant. Mac is a worker—always on the move—eager to put his hands to something. When the church needs a janitor, he takes the job gladly; he comes in after work and waxes the floors until midnight. Mac is the sort of fellow who seems to embody the biblical dictum "Whatsoever thy hand findeth to do, do it with thy might."

Once, when we're talking at church about our new Spanish-speaking neighbors—at a time when politicians have decided to build a wall on our country's southern border and call these people "illegal"—I throw out an idea to this congregation. The people here have a living memory of participating in the Civil Rights movement. I stand and say to them, "Why don't some of us go down to the borderlands, see what our neighbors are going through to get here, and learn how we might get involved in the immigration issue?" Folks nod and say, "Amen." But I'm a young white brother who often has an idea to pitch. The Civil Rights veterans who recount their stories every year during Black History Month are supportive, but they have other commitments. It's Mac and his older sister who step forward and say, "We'll go."

We do, and Mac keeps the group in stitches, laughing at himself—and all the rest of us—as we try to set up camp in the Arizona desert in the midst of a monsoon. He finds a lot to laugh about as we meet with a "Minuteman" who spews hate one minute and insists a moment later that he's not racist. "Hell, I'm married to a Mexican American," the self-styled patriot tells us. Humor, Mac knows from experience, is one way to relieve the incontrovertible tension of life inside a contradiction. You laugh and you pray, unable to imagine any way out but knowing this is not where you're supposed to be. Maybe, like Jonah, you'll find your feet on the ground again. But there's nothing you can do to make it happen. After you've poured yourself out in prayer, you listen to your own laughter echo through the belly of a whale.

After we cross over to Mexico with a "coyote" who used to guide economic refugees across the harsh desert landscape, he takes us to visit an addiction-recovery facility. It is a compound of small block houses, each crammed full of bed frames bunked three high. The men are thin, many of them dressed in little more than rags. Our guide tells us that these men try to find work as laborers, taking construction and janitorial jobs. United in need, they are trying to make a life together, to help one another get by with scant resources. They have nothing, but they worry about neighbors who have less. One of the men jumps on the truck to go with us as we leave to refill water tanks that they've set up in the desert for people who are crossing, in search of a better life.

I notice after our visit—after we have walked the desert trails, feeling the heat that has claimed thousands of lives over the past decade—that Mac is particularly quiet. His face is twisted, his gaze focused hard on nothing in particular. He is thinking about something.

"You all right?" I ask, and he shakes his head, still working through the conundrum that his typical laugh can't overcome. "Did you see those guys at that recovery shelter?" he asks. "I think I've got it bad," he says, "and then I see something like that."

When we are back home, Mac tells me that he's been saving up for a new mattress—a nice place to lay his head when the day's work is done. He prays every morning that his body will be tired when he comes to the end of the day. He hopes that having a good mattress would mean he'd be wrapped in sweet rest, a guard against the demons that whisper in the dark. But he keeps thinking about the guys across the border, sleeping three high on hard bunks.

"I'm sending this money to them," he tells me. "They need it more than I need a mattress."

Mac has been where these men are today. He sends the money as a prayer that somehow this old world might be set right—that the men with the hollow eyes might find life. He sends it because he never learned the middle-class habit of calculating every move. He does not check himself when he knows what should be done. Mac knows in his bones that we are put here for some purpose. Sure, we can get off track. Our twisted desires can trick us into thinking that a temporary high is the one great good, demanding nothing less than everything. But after you have seen through the scam—after you've experienced a temporary high, only to feel the floor fall out from beneath you—you still have to decide this: Were you wrong to plunge forward, no-holds-barred, toward the one thing that promised true joy? Or did you have your sights set too low? Mac decides to aim a little higher—to go after a greater good—but he's still going to give it all he's got.

One evening as I sweep the front porch, I notice that Mac is carrying boxes from his apartment to a truck across the street. "Looks like you're moving," I say. "What's up?"

"I'm going back to the mission," he tells me, referring to the residential recovery program that he checked himself into a few years back. "I need a few months to get my head straight. I know I can't do this thing on my own." I ask what he's planning after that, and he says he's not sure—that he's taking it one step at a time. "Well," I tell him, "you give us a call if you'd like to come to Rutba House. You know you're welcome."

When he calls, Mac says he'd like to try staying here for a few months. "You know we don't have TV," I remind him. He laughs. "Yeah, I know." And then he says this: "But I know I don't need to be on my own." This realization is enough to send him plunging headlong into the midst of our crazy life together. He never gives it a second thought.

I don't realize it at the time, and I don't begin to understand It until he has been part of our family for years: Mac helps raise our kids and is with us to weather the storms of life. He weeps with us when we lose Leah's mother, not just because his friends are hurting but also because he knows what it's like to lose a mother. I don't realize it, but Mac is our Jonah, spit out on the shoreline of our life, preaching a one-line sermon that is an invitation to new life. "I know I don't need to be on my own," he proclaims. It is a call to repentance. Mac has come to save us from our habit of independence, to teach us to run with all we've got toward the all-consuming higher good of real community.

In a scholarly study of addiction and its implications for ethical thought, I find a line that jumps off the page because it names what I have seen: "Persons with severe addictions are among those contemporary prophets that we ignore to our own demise, for they show us who we truly are."

Five

Battle Scars

One fall afternoon when things are feeling fairly hopeful, I get a call from Freedom House, a recovery community for people who struggle with drugs and alcohol. They have a guy who doesn't quite fit their program but seems serious about dealing with his alcoholism. Might we have space for him?

Doc comes to dinner that evening, then sits on the front porch and talks for an hour afterward. We show him a room that's vacant and invite him to try it out for a couple of weeks.

"I'll have to find some way to get all my stuff over here," Doc says. I ask him what kind of stuff we're talking about. "You know, things you can keep outside, mostly. For my work." I end up renting a U-Haul to pick up a homeless man. Doc gives me an address outside town where I can meet him. I've driven this road many times on the way to a friend's farm. But when I get to the intersection just beyond which I am to find a driveway, I see nothing but woods. *Did I write this down wrong?*

I pass the drive only to notice in my rearview mirror a small orange cone in the easement that Doc had mentioned. I turn around and go back. There is—or, rather, there used to be—a dirt road by this little cone. It is overgrown, the branches of pine trees covering its opening in the tree line. Slowly, I push through limbs with the U-Haul, praying that I won't have to pay for the scratches I hear being made along the sides of the truck.

About a quarter mile into the woods, I find a cabin. No electricity or running water, just log walls and a tin roof. It's definitely off the grid. And off the beaten path. I've seen enough scary movies that my blood pressure is up. I notice the Confederate flag tacked up on the side of the cabin. It is weathered, but it is the only decoration on this dark and lonesome shack.

Doc steps out of the cabin in jeans, an old T-shirt, and a baseball cap bearing the US Marine Corps insignia. I learn later that he spent eight years as a marine, dropping into Central America and Lebanon for low-intensity combat. "I learned to live simple," he'll tell me. "Don't need much." But on this fall day, through the window of a U-Haul truck, Doc looks every bit like a man from another time. He could have been living in these woods since 1865.

Outside the cabin Doc has lined up his personal belongings packed in liquor boxes—some clothes, a box of books, tools and engraving equipment, several wooden signs, and dozens of potted plants. "I'm a horticulturalist," Doc tells me, his eyes bright. "Maybe we can get a greenhouse started over there at the house." We pack up, jump in the truck, and drive back to town, listening to a country music station. I like Doc. He reminds me of my uncles from the North Carolina mountains.

Most everyone else likes Doc too. He has his quirks, like a habit of drinking a dozen cups of instant coffee a day and the ability to fit jalapeño peppers into any meal. But he's easy to get along with, makes a mean barbecue chicken on his cooking night, and shows up faithfully for prayers every morning. "Man, I need this," Doc tells me. "You just don't know." But I do know. Because I need it too.

Doc settles into the healing rhythm of life together that we inherited from fifteen hundred years of monastic communities: pray together, eat together, work in between. He's an artist with a long, complicated story about why the feds garnish his wages if he works a job on the books. So Doc sets up shop on our back porch, engraving wooden signs that he sells in parking lots outside college football games. He can freehand Duke's Blue Devil and the University of North Carolina's ram. When it comes to sports teams, he's an equal-opportunity propagandist. But we notice that his political humor leans significantly to the right of center.

One afternoon when I'm in the kitchen, Mac asks if I've seen the back porch in the past few days. No, I've not been back there, I tell him. But I gather I should have a look. Above his work station Doc has tacked his full-size Confederate flag to the wall. Beneath it I notice a sign that reads Obama bin Lying.

We need to talk about things. Dan, another member of the house, and I invite Doc to join us for breakfast the next weekend. Like me, Dan grew up in rural North Carolina. But he was never a good ol' boy. Dan's parents had relocated from Minnesota. On top of that, they were Catholic. He remembers learning as a kid that the Ku Klux Klan hated people like him as much as they hated black folks.

At breakfast Dan begins by saying, "I know you may not mean to be offensive, but we live in an African American neighborhood. When our neighbors see your Confederate flag, they see hate." Doc seems genuinely confused. "Y'all know I can get along with anybody," he says with a broad smile. "I ain't gonna let a little politics get between me and my neighbor."

I decide to weigh in. "Look, I grew up around here. I know boys that fly the Stars and Bars, and I know what kind of guns they keep behind the seat of their pickup trucks." We go on like this for half an hour, only to arrive at an ultimatum: It's our house. If he wants to stay, he'll take the flag and the signs down. He does, but the war rages inside him. It isn't long before Doc has had a relapse with alcohol and is living on the street again.

Among the homeless who live on the streets, veterans are fairly common. But knowing Doc gets me to thinking about homelessness as one of the scars of war—even more than a century after a war that continues to mark this region. In 1865, after Confederate troops surrendered at Bennett Place here in Durham, Johnny went marching north with sacks full of the gold leaf tobacco he had enjoyed around campfires as the Civil War wound down. With little other good news to report, Union soldiers sang the praises of this flavorful, wide-leaf weed. When the supply in their sacks ran out, they sent down South for more. The farmers of North Carolina were happy to oblige. If nicotine helped soothe the souls of boys who'd gone home scarred, their cash served to soften the pain of this place. Durham grew up on tobacco money, rose out of the ashes of the Civil War.

When you're trying to pick up the pieces of your life after your backyard has been a battlefield, I guess any money seems like progress. But in and of itself, money is no better a fix than drugs for the wounds that war exposes. Durham did not become a place where black and white folks made life together in the postbellum South because they had made their peace. Durham became a diverse and messy cross section of the South because there were jobs here.

By the turn of the twentieth century, the American Tobacco Company, headed by James B. Duke, was the largest corporation in the world. By the turn of the twenty-first century,
when we showed up in Walltown, Mr. Duke's name was
stamped on the university and hospital system that employ
more of Durham than any other local business. But the growth
of cities such as Durham following the Civil War cannot be
understood apart from the story of homelessness in America,
because the story of southern men such as James B. Duke is tied
to the stories of men like Doc.

In his landmark history of homelessness, *Down and Out,
on the Road,* Kenneth Kusmer notes that "in the immediate
postwar period, a considerable number of former soldiers slid
into a life of vagrancy or petty crime. Prison officials in Mas-
sachusetts, Pennsylvania, and Illinois found that two-thirds
of their charges in 1866 and 1867 were veterans." The reasons
were many: a recession followed the war; soldiers who had
learned to ride the railroads were suddenly mobile; having
camped for years, many veterans found it easier to just go on
living outside. (Doc: "I learned how to live simple.") But beneath these changing circumstances lay a deeper reason—a
hidden wound in the soul of the nation. "A house divided
against itself cannot stand," Abraham Lincoln had said.
When the fighting was over, many found they had nowhere
to go home to.

Kusmer notes that terms such as *bum* and *tramp* began to appear in American newspapers for the first time in the late 1860s. While antivagrancy laws had been on the books in many places since the late eighteenth century, the Civil War gave America the homeless as a new class of people. From both sides of the battle, hollow men who had fought a war in which there were no winners wandered the face of the earth, searching for a place to belong. Their homelessness became a living sign that, in so many ways, the war never really ended.

The sins of the fathers are visited upon their children, even to the fourth and fifth generation. You see it in a guy like Doc, whose alcoholism is fueled by lost-cause religion. When you pass him on an exit ramp several months later, holding a sign that reads Homeless Vet, Please Help, you can feel a hundred fifty years of history crying out, longing for someone to hear its lament. The "bum" who first showed up after the Civil War is with us still, not a half mile down I-85 from the road sign for Bennett Place.

The daughters and sons of James B. Duke can no more imagine a world without war than Doc can find his way home. We are, all of us, caught up in this history. Even if the good people of the New South pull down every monument to a Confederate soldier, men like Doc will still stand on our exit ramps, flesh-and-blood memorials to a wound that has not healed. To ignore them is to ignore the pain that fuels our violence.

The summer we move into Walltown, one of the guys who hangs out on a corner just down the street from Rutba House gets shot. In the middle of the day, someone from across town drives up, sticks a gun out the window of a car, and pulls the trigger. Isaac happens to be driving behind the car that carries the gunman. He stops his car, jumps out, and asks the guy who's been hit in the elbow if he needs a ride to the hospital. "Naw," this young man says, gritting his teeth and pressing his hand against the wound. "I'll be all right."

The next evening, the same car from across town shows up. This time the gunman takes better aim. The dogs howl all night, and the next morning the momma of the guy who now has been shot twice finds her son. He is facedown in an alley. We learn at his funeral that his name was Robert.

Fresh off our peacemaking journey to Iraq—high on the possibilities of enemy love—we want to respond to this tragedy with a nonviolent-action campaign. We want to call in the troops from Christian Peacemaker Teams and get in the way of these bullets, laying our bodies down to help young black men see that Martin Luther King Jr.'s notion of the beloved community wasn't just a pipe dream.

But Ray tells us what the guys on the street are saying. Some have us pegged as a police house, sent to monitor drug traffic. Others say we're a plant from Duke—part of a secret plan to take over the neighborhood. Who are we kidding? We're not the Special Forces unit in a nonviolent crusade for justice. To the guys on the corner, we look like a fresh crop of James B. Duke's descendants.

Which is to say, we are the enemy. What's missing here is not some Gandhi-like tactics that can be brought in from elsewhere but a basic trust. Truth is, the guys who conduct business on the corner know more about me than I know about them. I start trying to engage them in conversation. I learn their names, and they learn mine. A couple of them start coming by the house for dinner. Whenever I get a chance, I stop by their corner to catch up. One day a fellow named Andre, who likes to rap when he talks, says to me, "You want to talk theology, don't you?"

Andre has watched me walk back and forth to the Saint John's Missionary Baptist Church every Sunday and Wednesday for the past couple of years. He's part of the contingent that has decided we're not a police house or a university plant; we are the "church house." In his mind, the battle lines have been drawn in theological sand. He's got a point to make. "Well, I'm a Muslim," he raps, hands flying up and down:

I'm a Muslim because
Christianity's about
what you believe in your heart,

but Islam is about

how you live.

I'm a Christian who gets up every morning and goes to bed every night praying, "Thy kingdom come, thy will be done, on earth as it is in heaven." I live with people who want Christianity to shape our whole lives. But I cannot argue with Andre. The Christianity he has seen is too often a feel-good spirituality, a get-me-through-another-week kind of faith. "Crack religion," some folks around here call it. Andre prefers just plain crack to this pie-in-the-sky spirituality.

It is a gift to know people who keep it real, even when talking about faith. One day I say to a guy I've gotten to know well—a young man who's run the streets since he was thirteen—"Jesus said, 'If you live by the gun you'll die by the gun.'" There's no good use for a gun in this neighborhood, I tell him. It will get you killed, or it will land you in prison for shooting someone else. But he says to me, "You oughta tell that to the police." Jesus is well and good for the church house. But out here on the street, he says, religion can get you killed.

I think about the conversations I've had with Christian soldiers. Their realism has forced them to conclude that whatever Jesus meant when he said what he did about loving our enemies, he must not have meant it for people at war. As I listen to the guys on the corner, it occurs to me, *They think like soldiers.*

These guys are living in a war zone. The streets where they grew up playing football and riding bikes are the front lines of America's War on Drugs.

Trying to make sense of all of this, I learn that in the early 1980s, back when homelessness was first declared a public crisis, the Reagan administration decided that drugs were the evil at the root of urban America's problems. As the research money of the largest defense budget in history was being poured into nuclear deterrence, the guns and armored vehicles that had been designed for combat in Vietnam got redirected to local police departments. Federal programs offered city police large grants to purchase this equipment for their newly trained anti-drug units. Many of the men hired to head drug-law enforcement teams were Vietnam vets who knew the equipment well. Meanwhile, the guys who hang out on our corner grew up watching police raid crackhouses like they were hideouts for the Vietcong.

One summer afternoon when things are quiet around the house, I am reading at a desk in our back room. The window above is open, letting in a breeze. I look up from my reading because I hear an engine roaring, like I'm trackside at Charlotte Motor Speedway. Across our backyard, between two houses that face the next street, I watch first one police car then another race down the street. Then I hear an explosion. The desk trembles, and my muscle memory goes back to Baghdad in

2003, when for a few days my body learned what it's like to live beneath bombs. My instinct is to take cover.

But I remember I'm at home. I'm sitting at a desk in my house, a quarter mile from Duke University. So I run to the front porch. Police are converging outside of C-Lo's house, around the corner on the cross street. I walk to the corner, joining other neighbors who've come to see what's going on. A dozen pit bulls are running loose as two men pull up in an animal-control truck. A few minutes later, C-Lo is led out of his house, hands cuffed behind his back, escorted by two officers.

The explosion, I learn, was from concussion grenades, tossed through the windows to shock the people inside before a SWAT team stormed the house. The police considered the raid a success. No one was hurt. They found plenty of evidence to put C-Lo away for a long time on drug-trafficking charges. But this raid was a victory in the same way Operation Iraqi Freedom was. Yes, we got Saddam. But the Lord only knows how many children will have nightmares in Baghdad tonight, how many kids in Walltown will grow up knowing that the police are an enemy that might storm into your home at any time.

Maybe when your enemies are half a world away it's easier to forget them. Maybe it's possible to believe that the well-being of Iraqis or Afghanis doesn't have much to do with us. But the children of these police officers go to school with kids from Walltown. We pay for the ammo that disrupted our neighborhood this afternoon. Yes, we all try to identify who is on which side in any conflict. We recognize divisions of neighborhood, of race, of class. But war is notoriously imprecise. On the afternoon when our block is raided, standing with neighbors opposite the corner where the young guys usually hang out, I realize they are right: this is a war zone. Only in this war, we're bombing ourselves.

———

When Leah's cell phone rings on a Wednesday night, we're already in bed. It's Gary, the high-functioning quadriplegic who lives with us. We loaned our van to Blue, a friend of his, so they could go to a fast-food restaurant and get something to eat. Blue knows that it's the anniversary of Gary's mom's murder. He didn't want him to be alone.

I can tell from Leah's voice that something is wrong. Gary is asking where the registration form is in the van. They've been pulled over. She asks where they are, and I hear him give their location. "Tell him I'll be there in two minutes." I grab my tennis shoes and run around the corner in my pajamas.

By the time I get there, two patrol cars are lined up behind our van, their lights flashing. An officer is standing at each side of the van. I approach the one on the driver's side and tell him this is my van and I'd be glad to help them find anything they need. He asks me to wait on the sidewalk, where I begin to see what is happening. Three young black men in a van are parked under a streetlight in their own neighborhood, detained by two white officers—both about their age. I wonder if any of them went to high school together.

I see a neighbor step onto his porch. I walk over to talk to him about what's going on. We stand together, the two of us, on the sidewalk beside the first officer's patrol car. I memorize the ID numbers on the sides of the car and wait to see what happens.

When the officer walks back to his car, I ask what moving violation led him to stop the van. I know from the markings on his vehicle that he's a member of the HEAT, one of Durham's drug enforcement units. He's not out here to make routine traffic stops. He's hoping for a drug bust. But the easiest way to find drugs—the way to do search and seizure without a warrant— is to stop a moving vehicle. Technically, the officer is supposed to have some reason other than the fact that the minivan is being driven by a young black man. But it's not hard to come up with something. "I could tell you," the officer says to me, "but I won't. I'll let the driver tell you when we're done here."

After he's been in the patrol car for a few minutes, a K-9 unit pulls up, joining the line of vehicles. For some reason, the officer I've been interacting with decides to change his approach. He gets out of his car and comes over. "Gentlemen, I'm concerned about your safety," he says. "These guys are considered armed and dangerous. I want to encourage you to go back to your homes." I assure the officer that I'm not there because I'm worried about the guys in my van. I'm there to watch him. Red in the face, he resumes his search.

He asks Blue and another of Gary's friends, Shawn, to step out of the van. Another officer frisks them on the sidewalk. Gary, I gather, explains that he can't easily get out of the van without first getting into the wheelchair that is stored in the back. The officers let him stay in his seat while the dog is walked around our van, sniffing for drugs. The dog finds nothing, and after another ten minutes or so, the guys get back in the van and drive away.

"Your buddies didn't even stay to give you a ride," the officer says with a smirk. I haven't punched another guy in the face since junior high school, but I have a distinct memory of the feeling in my gut that preceded that action. I am feeling it now.

I walk into the street, setting my sights on home. "I'll talk to you after I've talked to your captain," I say.

"Go right ahead," he replies. "He'll thank me for doing my job."

Back at home I check in with Gary and his friends, who are not surprised by the interruption of their evening. "Man, they always doing shit like that," one of them says. As they help Gary get back into his bed, I sit at the kitchen table, composing a racial-profiling complaint, which I send to Durham's chief of police by e-mail. He responds the next morning, sending a lieutenant to take our statements and begin an investigation. Over the next few weeks, I will talk to her for hours. She is a thorough and generous woman who shares my faith and respects the work we do in the neighborhood. But when the investigation is done and she has filed her final report, her conclusion will be that the officer, while admittedly rude, didn't break any rules. Everything he did was within the law.

I know this will be the case, even as I write at the table, swinging words like I wanted to swing my fist just minutes earlier. I'm writing because I don't know what else to do—because even when you can't change a broken system, you can still insist that it is wrong. I hear the door to Gary's room open. I see Blue standing at the other end of the kitchen, shuffling back and forth. I stop typing and look at him. He's trying to find the words to say something.

"I'm sorry I couldn't do any more," I say to him. "I'm sorry you had to sit there and take that."

Blue crosses the room in three quick steps and throws his arms open, wrapping me in a bear hug before I can stand up. "Man, thanks for standing out there with us," he says. Then he steps back. He isn't sure what else to say, and I'm not either.

"I'll see you," he says. As he walks out the door, I see him reach with the back of his hand to wipe a tear from his cheek.

Six

The Prison Line

———

Jesus said, "I was a stranger and you welcomed me," but it turns out that most guests—even the strangest ones—don't come knocking without some introduction. A friend brings them by. A social worker calls. Their momma asks if they can stay here. Lives are complex, and no two stories are the same, but you learn to recognize in these introductory stories some common denominators. One of them is prison.

Prison is, in fact, so common to the stories of folks who become homeless that we begin to see how it draws a line between people, separating us like sheep from goats. There are, on the one side, those for whom prison is an unimaginable reality. On the other side are people for whom prison has always been part of their lives. Most of us who came here fresh from college are on the first side. Most of the guests who show up at our door live and move and have their being on the other side.

Early one Sunday morning, I drive to the Durham Correctional Center to pick up Greg. He's spent the past sixteen months at a state prison down east, working overtime in the kitchen so he could get out six weeks early. A few days ago, the Department of Corrections transferred him to this local minimum-security facility. Greg knows the place well. He's been released from here more times than he can count.

"Feel good to be out?" I ask as we walk through the gate of the chain-link fence, nodding good-bye to the guards. "You know it does," Greg says, his back straight and his eyes fixed on the horizon. He's smiling from ear to ear. I remember another friend, Franklin, who once scrambled to roll down the window when I picked him up from another minimum-security prison, one county over. He wasn't being released, just let out on a four-hour pass, a taste of freedom meant to prepare him for his return to society. He held his hand out the open window as I drove along the state highway at fifty-five miles per hour. "You don't know how good it feels to touch free air," he said. Greg doesn't say it, but his smile does. He's relishing this little taste of freedom.

Only, Greg knows that it is fleeting. Because as good as it might feel to walk through the gate, hop in a car, and hold your hand out in the breeze, guys like Greg know that leaving prison doesn't mean you get to leave this part of your life behind. Not even if you have been released.

On any given day, some 2.4 million Americans live behind bars. Three times that many people are caught up in the US criminal-justice system—if not behind bars, then checking in with a parole officer who has the power to send them back to jail any time they fail to comply fully with the rules that restrict their tenuous freedom. That's 3 percent of the adult population in this country. In a neighborhood like Walltown, it means someone from every family.

But even if you've done your time—even if you walk out the gate like Greg, time served—on every job application you still have to check the box that says you're a convicted felon. You still have to deal with the debts that piled up, ruining your credit while you were locked away. You still have to figure out what to do with relationships that were cut off because you spent the last decade behind bars.

Maybe it was because Ray was Miss Lewis's son—or maybe because he was so likable—but it didn't occur to me when we welcomed him, our first guest coming home from prison, that we were crossing a dividing line. It didn't occur to me until the reporter called to ask if we'd seen Ray's record. I knew then that the idea of people from opposite sides of this divide living together might strike some as not only peculiar but also offensive.

Dangerous, even. Years later, after we've welcomed a dozen ex-cons into our homes, a neighbor sends an anonymous e-mail. "You should think of your children. You should think of our children. You're not just endangering yourselves; you're putting us all at risk."

As much as the note makes my stomach clench—as angry as I am that this neighbor wouldn't talk to me directly, wouldn't even sign their name—I know that they are right about one thing: there is a risk in welcoming people who are coming out of prison. You might come home after a Thanksgiving celebration to find that all the laptops in your house are gone. You might learn, only years after it happened, that another guest's Social Security number was stolen—that he has been listed as a dependent on the tax returns of someone he never knew. When you learn these things, you will pray with everything in you that worse hasn't happened—that people you love are not carrying unspeakable wounds.

Even when you have contemplated the worst, you will know this: these dangers are not peculiar to living in close quarters with the formerly incarcerated. Yes, the risk may be greater with some people than others, and you'd be a fool not to account for that. But the dividing line between good and evil does not run between those who've been to prison and those who haven't. It cuts through the center of every soul.

You know this too because you've lived with guys like Ray

and Greg and Franklin. You know this because they've helped you see how, in so many ways, you're not that different from them. This distance between you was decreed, of course, for the best of reasons—to protect you, to rehabilitate them. But prison bars have a way of playing with our imagination. Like a premature judgment day, they separate people marked "criminal" from the rest of society, creating a cast of characters (the antagonists) who are forced to live without hope and a future. Prison is an institution, not unlike the race-based slavery of our past, which somehow teaches us to see some people as essentially different from others.

In 1903, as he watched racism morph following America's Civil War, W. E. B. Du Bois wrote, "The problem of the Twentieth Century is the problem of the color line." A hundred years later, opening your door to people who are coming home from prison, you see how America's original sin has morphed again, but it is with us just the same. The problem of our own century is the problem of the prison line.

Prison matters not just for those who've been there, but for all of us. Back in college, when I read many things I didn't entirely understand, I came across a line from Dostoevsky: "The degree of civilization in a society can be judged by entering its prisons."

Here at Rutba House I begin to suspect that Dostoevsky was right—that he was, in fact, saying more than I can understand. This writer of Russian classics, like so many of the people we host, spent time in prison. From the inside, prison is a particular sort of window on our world.

Recidivism is the official label given to the tendency of people who've been in prison to end up there again. Most efforts to curb this tide are focused on helping individuals make better choices. When Greg gets arrested for stealing a paintbrush one night, I'm pissed off. *Why the heck would he steal a paintbrush?* But recidivism is about more than stupid choices—about more than individuals who need to do the right thing. Because there are plenty of places where picking up a neighbor's paintbrush when you've had too much to drink isn't going to land you in jail. When we get Greg's first letter, after he was picked up for petty theft of a paintbrush, he tells us he's facing twelve years as a repeat offender. *Twelve years for a five-dollar item?*

That letter tells us, as every friend's first letter does, which visitation day Greg has been assigned. Each inmate at our county jail can have four people on his visitation list. Once the inmate is sentenced to serve time in prison, the limitations are similar, only there a visitor cannot be on more than one inmate's list, unless they're immediate family. Because of these rules—and because everyone only has so much time—we split up the visitors. Leah takes Greg; I take Rodney. Matt, another member of Rutba House, takes Junior. Eventually, everyone in our little community of a dozen or so people is writing or visiting someone who's locked up. We call their names at morning prayer. We send them books. When we can, we try to see them. These are our small steps across the prison line.

But this going in and out—this knowing and loving people who are going in and out—opens our eyes to the disturbing realities of our prison system. A guy named Mike says it as succinctly as anyone. One summer, he and I sit with a small group once a week inside a prison library, talking about the books we're reading. After he's released, Mike writes to say, "Those couple of hours in the library each week—they were the only time when I was locked up that I felt like a human being."

It's not a single relationship—it's no one particular incident—but rather the cumulative effect of living back and forth across the prison line that begins to work on us. Whatever abstract thoughts any of us had about prison before are now distilled by the difficult stories of people we can't ignore—people who've eaten at our table and gone on vacation with our families. Yes, they can be frustratingly selfish and annoying as hell. Some of them have done terrible things, and as much as they regret them, they might well do them again if they were put in the same situation. These people are not angels. But they are people, for heaven's sake.

Once, our friend Marcia calls to tell us about a guy named

Al, a guy she met through a reentry ministry that she helped start. (It is her personal mission to stop gun violence in our town.) Rarely do you find in a determined activist someone with a heart as big as Marcia's. She is the sort of mother who, having raised her children, is somehow able to see them in anyone who has a need. Al is just wonderful, she tells us, but he's sharing a room with a guy who's using drugs. She would hate to see anything happen to him. Is there any way we might help? It's hard to say no to Marcia. Matt makes room on his top bunk, and Al moves in that week.

It turns out that Marcia is right: Al's great. He cleans up after himself, is always courteous, helps out around the house, even lands a job a couple of miles away that he walks to when he can't catch a ride. I run into Marcia at a meeting downtown and tell her she's sent us the model guest. "Oh, I know," she beams. "Isn't he just wonderful?"

How, I begin to wonder, did a guy like Al end up in prison? One night at our kitchen table he tells me the story. As a young black man in New York City, he had struggled to find work that would pay the bills. He kept his eyes open, of course. Al wasn't lazy; he was always on the move. But his options seemed so limited.

A friend told him about a place where you could sell a laptop computer for one hundred dollars, no questions asked. "Are you serious?" he asked. Al's the type of guy who notices things.

"Every coffee shop in Manhattan is *full* of laptops." Al started making a good living off college students who thought they could just run to the bathroom real quick while writing a paper at Starbucks.

After several months of this, Al was sitting in his apartment looking at a laptop he'd stolen. He noticed the sticker on the bottom had a phone number to call for technical assistance. He dialed the number, asked a few questions about hardware, and then asked, "Where are these things made anyway?" He jotted "Research Triangle Park" on a piece of paper, and the wheels started spinning. The next day, when Al took the laptop to his buyer, he asked him, "What would you give me if I brought you a whole truckload full of these?"

"Same price," the guy said. "A hundred bucks apiece."

Al recruited friends he could trust to help him. He researched what security was like at this factory. He found out who would be in the building and when. He rented a U-Haul truck, picked up his three co-conspirators, and drove to North Carolina, arriving at the factory late on a weekend night. Wearing a ski mask and wielding a handgun, Al burst into the factory, got all the employees together in one office, and tied them to chairs.

In the chaos of these intense minutes, a middle-aged African American woman started freaking out. She was screaming, "Please don't kill me" and starting to hyperventilate. Al couldn't help but think how much she looked like his mother. He wheeled her to the side, pulled back his ski mask, and said, "Look at me. I ain't gonna hurt you. Please just sit in this room until we're gone. The police will come in a few minutes and let you out."

She quieted down. Al and his friends loaded the truck, and in thirty minutes they were headed north on I-85. Just after they crossed the New Jersey line, Al noticed blue lights flashing in his rearview mirror. He looked down and saw that he was speeding. "All right, everybody stay calm," he said. "I'll handle this." But before he could stop the van on the shoulder of the highway, one of his buddies was rolling out of the passenger-side door. The man jumped the guardrail to make a break for it, and the highway patrolman noticed and called for backup. Al ended up doing ten years in prison.

I am caught up in his story. *What an idiot his friend was,* I think. *They almost got away.* But this isn't an action movie that's got my blood pressure up. It's Al's life. He's had ten years to tell and retell the story, and he has the timing down just right. He knows it's entertaining. "You should write a novel," I tell him, and he smiles. But the fun of telling his story is bittersweet. Because Al also knows it cost him everything. Once you've crossed the prison line, you're marked for life.

Later that night when I'm trying to go to sleep, I think about my buddy Marty. We grew up together, even got to see some of the world with each other when we were teenagers. When we get together now, we sit around after the kids have gone to bed and tell stories about the stupid things we did, mostly without getting caught. No, we never held anyone at gunpoint. But I'm not sure Al would have either if he had, like Marty and me, gone off to college, married, and settled down someplace with a job that was challenging enough to contain his imagination.

All of us are made by the little things that take place in our lives. Al is nothing like Marty. The two men, both good friends of mine, lived completely different lives. But I can't help thinking that, given different circumstances, Al might be an old friend from childhood, stopping by with his family, telling stories about the crazy things we did when we were kids.

That isn't his story though. Al grew up in a different world. He is a convicted felon, and he doesn't try to deny that. But he is much more than that. Just like all of us are more than the stupidest thing we ever did. At our best, we know we are more than just one unfortunate fact from our past. At our best, we can tell the stories and laugh at ourselves.

When we read in the newspaper that an execution is scheduled for early Friday morning at Central Prison in Raleigh, some of us drive over and join a small group of people gathered outside to pray. We make this trip a few times before we realize an execution is being scheduled every other week. Our state is killing people who are not unlike the friends we've hosted at Rutba House—people whom we suspect might be Jesus, hard as it is to see sometimes.

The bizarre thing—the realization that makes me shiver—is that our state also seems to recognize Jesus in the people who are marked for execution. In a strangely familiar ritual, the official protocol pays lip service to this irony. The man marked for death is served a last supper on Thursday evening, his final appeals are made to authorities through the night, and he is marched to the death chamber early Friday morning. Our representatives in government are playing Pontius Pilate, and there are Roman soldiers present in a cruel reenactment of Christ's Passion Week. Sitting vigil outside the prison gates, we sing "Were You There When They Crucified My Lord?"

Several times we are there to the bitter end, praying and asking ourselves how in the world this makes sense to anyone. Then I recall statements from victims' family members that I've read in the paper. I think about what it would feel like to lose my wife, my brother, my mother to senseless violence.

I can't imagine the pain that is experienced by those who lost a loved one, but I can completely understand their anger. Still, as I watch fellow citizens walk into the prison, there to witness the murder of their loved one's murderer, I can only pray, "Lord, have mercy."

I've been going to church and hearing sermons about Jesus all my life, but nothing makes the message of the Cross as clear to me as this scene outside the death house. Either Jesus died and rose again to put a stop to this cycle of so-called redemptive violence, or the whole story is just a bunch of wishful thinking about the sweet by-and-by.

We choose to keep trusting Jesus, which means we have to do something. These executions, we start to say, are idolatrous. They are a sacrifice made to a vengeful god that continues to demand more and more blood in exchange for our false sense of security. And they are being carried out in our name.

It is Lent, the season when Christians traditionally make public signs of penance, asking forgiveness for our sins. On Ash Wednesday, we receive the cross-shaped smudge on our foreheads and wear it throughout the day as a sign that we remember we are dust and to the dust we shall return. This year, when we receive our ashes, everyone at Rutba House also pins onto our shirts a scarlet letter *I* for idolatry. We wear the *I* for forty days, passing out slips of paper explaining our objections to the death penalty to anyone who asks.

But it is not this symbolic action against state-sponsored murder that lands us in jail. Executions continue at a rate of roughly one per fortnight, the seemingly inevitable result of a system that will tolerate protest but shows no sign of change. I recall Dietrich Bonhoeffer, the German theologian and pastor who openly opposed Hitler's barbarism. Bonhoeffer outlined succinctly at the beginning of Hitler's rise to power the available options for a church that objects to the practices of the state. Concerned Christians can, first, speak truth to power. What's more, they can and must care for the victims of a broken system. But, Bonhoeffer insisted, it is not enough to simply care for those who are being crushed under the wheel of an unjust regime. The time comes, he wrote, when we must "jam a spoke in the wheel."

For us, that time is the thousandth execution since the death penalty was reinstated in America. For a brief period in the 1970s, the US Supreme Court decided that killing a human being to demonstrate that the state will not tolerate murder was in violation of the US Constitution. State-sanctioned murder was found to be "cruel and unusual punishment." But a couple of years later, ruling in the case of *Gregg v. Georgia,* the court reversed its earlier decision, and in 1977 Gary Gilmore was executed by firing squad. Nine hundred ninety-eight people have been killed in execution chambers since then, and Kenneth Lee Boyd is scheduled to be the thousandth. He will die, according to the protocol, on the first Friday morning in December at North Carolina's Central Prison.

To mark this milestone, anti-death-penalty activists from

around the country will join us for our vigil. We meet with some of them the night before and make a plan for direct action. Before the required witnesses arrive to enter the prison, we will approach the guards and tell them we have come to stop the sacrifice that has been planned in our name. We will ask them to join us. When they refuse, we will put on sackcloth and ashes—the traditional signs of public penance among the Hebrew prophets— and kneel down to block the doors of the prison. We will refuse to move, making our bodies the spoke in this wheel.

At three o'clock on the morning of the scheduled execution, the guards are taken aback by our invitation. After years of standing in the cold, watching peaceful people hold candles and sing while someone is killed inside the building, they do not see this coming. They cannot join us, they say, nor can they let us proceed any farther. We must return to the designated protest area. But we can't. We don our burlap sacks, pull Ziploc bags of ashes from our pockets, and begin reading lines from the book of Lamentations:

> To crush underfoot
>   all prisoners in the land,
> to deny people their rights
>   before the Most High,
> to deprive them of justice—
>   would not the Lord see such things?

Beside me on his knees—his head bowed, his hands clutching a half page of verses—Shujaa reads in a steady voice. Just last night, in the living room of a sister hospitality house, Shujaa told me how he had been framed for the murder of a prison guard and sentenced to death at San Quentin in the seventies. Though he insisted on his innocence and there was no material evidence connecting him to the murder, Shujaa was already a convicted felon when he was accused. He was presumed guilty. It took four trials and nothing short of a miracle for him to prove his innocence. All that time—more than three years in all—he sat vigil in a death-row cell, watching others go to the death chamber as he prayed for justice. He wasn't sure what else he could do.

Would not the Lord see such things? Every time the guards walked a man to deathwatch, Shujaa wondered if he would be next.

My eyes will flow unceasingly,
   without relief,
until the LORD looks down
   from heaven and sees.
What I see brings grief to my soul.

I am holding the verses close to my face with one hand as I use the other to shake the opened Ziploc bag over my head.

The smell of ash fills my nostrils, and I strain to read the paper as the dim light of streetlamps filters through a cloud of dust. Shujaa almost died thirty-five years ago, strapped to a chair with high-voltage current burning his body.

Kenneth Lee Boyd is scheduled to die tonight. I haven't the slightest idea what it feels like to be marked for death, but I've begun to feel what it's like to be on the wrong side of the prison line, on the wrong side of the law. I am blocking the prison entrance. I have refused to follow the direct orders of police officers. Two officers lift me to my feet, pull my arms behind my back, and clamp handcuffs around my wrists. They walk me to a transport bus that is parked beside the prison, escort me to a seat near the back. I sit down beside Shujaa, who is staring intently out the window.

"You all right?" I ask.

"Yeah," he says, taking a deep breath. "This is the first time I've been in handcuffs since I left San Quentin."

After we're booked at the jail downtown, the magistrate allows us to sign ourselves out with a promise to appear in court three months from now. It's 3:30 a.m., and we are free to go home. But Kenneth Lee Boyd is dead. Another man is scheduled to die just after the New Year—and a few weeks after him, another. I learn these men's stories, even meet some of their family members who are begging the governor to spare their lives. But I can only think of Shujaa, sitting beside me in that bus just as powerless as he was during the years he sat on death row, wondering if he would die.

No, not everyone is innocent—not everyone on the row could get out, find a job, get married, and spend the rest of their lives serving others like Shujaa has done. But his life is all the proof I need that no one is beyond redemption, that the transforming power of love can cross even the prison line. It's Shujaa who I think of more than anyone else as I go back to every execution for the next several months, kneel down outside the gate of Central Prison, and watch hours slip by, praying that the Lord will look down from heaven and see. I get arrested every time.

The fifth time this happens, the authorities decide they've had enough. After they've photographed and fingerprinted us, they send us to the magistrate who says we're each being held under a five-thousand-dollar bond. An officer escorts me to a cell. Through an opening I am handed a large plastic bag that will hold my clothes. I am also handed an orange jumpsuit, a pair of boxers, and some flip-flops. The officer stands guard while I change, then walks me to a holding cell, where I join about a dozen other men who have also been arrested that night.

The corners of this twelve-by-twelve enclosure are taken by men who are trying to get a little sleep on wooden benches against cinder-block walls. I can't imagine sleeping beneath the fluorescent lights, but I guess if you're tired enough, you can sleep most anywhere. It's the middle of the night, but not everyone is sleeping. I find an open spot on a bench, my back against the wall, and watch a man in his midtwenties across from me who is detoxing. With his head down between his knees, his body is convulsing. A guard brings him some BC Powder, which he snorts like a line of cocaine. His head drops down again, and I watch saliva fall from his mouth.

When I'm finally sent upstairs to a cellblock, a guard walks me into a room where I'm issued a multicolored trifold mat. I note that it's similar to the one I used for nap time in kindergarten. Due to overcrowding, the officer tells me, this mat is my bunk. "Find a spot for it on the floor in the common area. Whenever we call count, make sure you're on it."

I step onto the cellblock, a small courtyard surrounded by double-occupancy cells stacked two stories high. A set of stairs stands halfway down the courtyard on the left, leading to a catwalk that circles the block. I feel like I'm in the gym at the community rec center back in Walltown, only no one is exercising on the track upstairs and the court is littered with tables, chairs, and sleep mats.

When I find a spot in a corner, the guy next to me looks me up and down and asks, "What the hell you doing here?" I tell him about the execution the night before—how some of us had knelt on the ground and tried to block the door—and he immediately stands up. "Hey, y'all ain't gonna believe this," he shouts. Then he gives a one-sentence summary of our action, complete with three expletives. I happened to sit down beside the unofficial leader of this block. He decides to lead an all-block rap session on executions and the criminal-justice system.

"Look around this room," he says to me, his eyes both earnest and angry. "I knew every guy in this place before we ever got here. We're all from the same zip code," he says, pointing a finger for emphasis. "The train that ends at death row starts here." He is looking at me. He knows I'm not supposed to be here, but somehow I am. What's more, he knows that I won't be here long. But if I'm going to take anything out of here with me, he wants to make sure I know this: a young black man who grows up on the other side of the prison line knows in his gut that he's caught up in a system that has marked him for death.

———

Walltown is one of the zip codes where the train starts. I realize that I have crossed the prison line—that I am caught up in our terribly broken criminal-justice system—because I share life with folks at Rutba House who are trying to get off the train. After my experience in jail, I realize that I keep talking about the education I gained on the cellblock. As I talked with those guys, both our common humanity and our need to struggle for justice together were clear to everyone. We need more spaces like that, I say. We need to help people outside get into prison— to see society from behind bars, to know people there as fellow human beings. I say it over and over again, not exactly sure what I mean.

Sarah, who has an uncanny gift for getting things done, has just had her first baby. She's excited about being a mom, but she has it all figured out in a couple of months. She's starting to get a little bored. I ask if she'd like to do something with this prison-based education idea. Maybe ten hours a week. She runs with it. Pretty soon she has graduate-level courses taught by tenured faculty running inside two state and one federal facility. Project TURN, she calls it. Every class roll is half students who are incarcerated and half students from outside the facility.

One afternoon, Sarah calls from the prison where she is teaching. Julie, a woman who's been incarcerated for twenty years—a woman who has taken a few TURN classes—has just learned she is being paroled. She has a spot reserved in a reentry program that starts in three months, but just now she found out she has to leave prison. Today.

Our system of mass incarceration is not set up to care for people like Julie. Though nothing of this exit plan was communicated to her until today, it is all within the law. She is expected to get in a car, ride to the county of her infraction—a place she hasn't visited in twenty years—and get out of the car on a street corner. This, according to the system, should be good news. Julie is going home early.

But it is not good news. Julie's case is complicated by the fact that, due to the nature of the plea that she agreed to sign, she is registered as a sex offender. She had reported her husband for child abuse, and complications arose from the way the system is set up and led to her being added to the registry. This does not mean that she sexually abused a child or that she would ever think of hurting anyone. But it does mean that Julie's name is on a list that makes everyone think she did. She cannot live in a household with children or within one thousand feet of a school or day care facility. That counts out all of our houses in Walltown, as well as most of the friends we know who are willing to welcome prisoners into their homes.

This is the conundrum that Sarah and I are discussing when, after a long pause, she says to me, "Call if you think of anything. I'm going to call some other folks." Like I said, Sarah doesn't dillydally. Not knowing what else to do, she starts going down her list of people who might help. For every answered phone, an apology. And a no.

Then, in a moment of desperation, Sarah picks up the list of women who have come into the prison over the past year to take a TURN course. Graduate students, they're mostly single.

She decides to give them a try. Within an hour, two of them who are roommates call back to say, "Yes. Of course we'll host Julie. Just tell us when she'll be here."

A few days later, when Sarah and I have a chance to catch up, I ask about Julie. As it happens, Julie got a one-week extension and was able to go straight to the reentry program that had already been lined up. But Julie is an exception. She is someone who had folks advocating for her. She is, as much as anyone, a reminder that the problem of our century is the problem of the prison line. But she and the grad students who were ready to welcome her are also an interruption to our broken system. Maybe something new becomes possible for those who cross the line. Maybe the guest coming home from prison shows up to invite you to reimagine your world.

Seven

Beside the Healing Pool

Though she isn't technically homeless—not anymore, at least—Lucille is the poorest person I've ever known. We meet her when she and her uncle Bobby are living as squatters in the old boardinghouse around the corner. Lucille is a perennially sick chain smoker who swears she "never eats hardly anything, just a bite here and there." The little food we carry over from the monthly food bank is hardly enough to keep two people alive, but I begin to wonder who eats it. Though Bobby goes out to beg on the corner, Lucille stays locked inside their single room like some desert ascetic. After knowing her for years, I realize that I've never seen her eat.

So I am surprised one day when I stop by and Lucille is poking her hand out the door, giving me five dollars and asking if I might go by the grocery store and get a bag of frozen chicken. This is, clearly, a precious five dollars. I ask to make sure I've got the order right. "Legs and thighs," Lucille says, coughing between breaths. "The frozen ones are cheaper. Them dogs love 'em. They won't eat nothin' else."

I hear a chorus of seven dogs barking behind her. This woman who hardly eats anything gives most of her food to canine companions who share a room with her and her aging uncle in an abandoned boardinghouse.

Some months later, when the deceased landlord's estate has been settled and the new owner realizes a couple of homeless people have been squatting in his house, I borrow a friend's truck and go over with a couple of volunteers to help Lucille and Bobby move. With some help from social services, they've been able to arrange for a small house, complete with running water and electricity. A homeless man and woman who used to sleep in the woods are getting a home. They and their seven dogs, two cats, and a bird.

When the door of their boardinghouse room is fully opened, the stench hits me with the impact of a wave. I force myself to keep my head up, to focus on the task at hand. When it's over, I go home, undress on the porch outside our house, and take a hot shower before I throw my soiled clothes away. Three days later I finally get the smell out of my nostrils.

This process is repeated about every nine months for the next seven years. Lucille calls to say she's getting evicted, we scramble to help her find a new place, and I recruit a couple of unsuspecting volunteers—never the same people twice—to help. I warn people, but there is no way that a warning can prepare a new recruit. Everyone who helps Lucille and Bobby move admits when it's over that they never could have imagined it in advance.

The problem, of course, is that two people who are both dirt poor and sick cannot take care of ten animals. They cannot take care of themselves. We try to bring this up with Lucille— Leah is better at it than I am. But Lucille always cuts us off with the same response: "Them dogs is all I got." This line is delivered with a desperate force that makes its logic seem unassailable.

But during one move, when it's just Quinton and me with a U-Haul truck, both of us coughing our lungs out as we kick the cockroaches off our pant legs, I lose my patience. We've been wading through pools of urine for an hour, trying to salvage what we can and get out. This place, like a dozen others, will be gutted as soon as we're gone. When we have the essentials loaded onto the truck, I ask Lucille to come outside. These animals, I say, are killing her. That cough that never goes away—it's not a smoker's cough. It's a direct result of breathing cockroach excrement. It will never go away until she gets rid of these animals.

I tell Lucille that we love her. She knows we do. We've been doing this for years. But I'm not going to watch her kill herself. I'm moving her stuff to the new place, but I'm not moving the dogs. She can decide whether to get in the truck with us and all her earthly possessions or stay in a rotting house with her dogs.

Lucille stays with the dogs. By the time I get to the new place, Leah has called on my cell phone. "What happened?" she asks. I give my version of the events—more colorful, perhaps, than the account above, but covering the same details—then pause because I'm not sure what else to say. Quinton and I are still coughing, both windows down in the cab of the U-Haul truck. "Dang," Quinton says, "I can't believe anybody lives like that." All Quinton has ever known is poor, but this is extreme, even for him.

Later that night, after I've showered twice and calmed down enough to listen, Leah tells me that Lucille called someone from the animal protection society who came and got her and the dogs and carried them to her new place. "I just can't believe Jonathan would do that," Lucille said. She was crying when she said it. "He knows them dogs is all I got."

Over the years, Lucille has told me the story of how she came to Durham in the late 1980s with a child who was dying from cancer. When this city that was built on tobacco began to transition to its postindustrial identity, it became the City of Medicine, drawing people from throughout the region to its three major hospitals. This city that grew by selling cigarettes to the world has been sustained by treating those same people's cancer. In Lucille's case, her son had leukemia. Lucille left home and spent every dime she had to try to save him. But she couldn't. She lost her only child and everything else besides.

When she was living in the woods out by the train tracks, Lucille found a little dog. It was a mutt, but she called him Freddie and taught him to smoke a cigarette. I have seen it with my own eyes. Freddie sits back on his haunches, holds the thing between his front two paws, and smokes like it's the most natural thing in the world. "That's my Freddie," Lucille says. When she watches him, she almost seems happy.

At some point Freddie and Lucille moved out of the woods and in with her uncle Bobby. They made a life together, taking in other dogs and keeping the puppies. Since Bobby died, Lucille has kept going, one day at a time, learning how to get by without the little income Bobby used to bring in from begging. "Them dogs is all I got," she says. And it's almost true.

I know all this as I lie in bed, long after Leah and I have finished talking about it. I need to go to sleep. I have to get up early to catch a flight to Canada, where I'm scheduled to speak at a conference about the love of Jesus. But I can't stop thinking about Lucille. I can't stop smelling her life.

In the Gospels there is a story about the pool at Bethesda—a fancy pool, they say, with five gazebos around it where sick people gathered, hoping to be healed. I can't imagine the scene without thinking of the waiting room at Duke Hospital. They recently built a brand-new cancer ward, complete with recliners next to picture windows for folks who are taking chemo. I've read that the waiting areas by the pool at Bethesda were there because people believed that healing was possible when the waters stirred. You just had to be there at the right moment to get in. Sick people gathered by the pool, waiting for their appointment, hoping against hope that this treatment would heal them.

But a lot of the people never got into the water.

As we have answered our door over the years, we learn in this City of Medicine that we are living by a healing pool. As it was in ancient Bethesda, so it is now. The sick and the lame wait, spending what little they have to get here, praying it will buy them the opportunity to be seen. But the promise of miraculous medicine, like the stirring of ancient waters, doesn't always pay off. Some are always left homeless, waiting to be healed.

Once we've been at this a while, social workers tell one another about Rutba House. One time, on a whim, a woman who works for Jewish Family Services—a woman who knows next to nothing about us—calls because she's desperate. She's up to her neck in a scenario they never covered in her MSW program. A friend once told her that in strange situations, the Rutba House might be able to help. She put our number in her

Rolodex. It just so happens that this time we're able to say yes. Never mind that we've had to say no a dozen times this year. The first time this woman calls, we say yes. She thinks we walk on water.

So one afternoon a few months later, I listen to a voice mail from one of her friends. This social worker is calling from the burn unit at the hospital. Her friend at Jewish Family Services thought we might be able to help. When a knock comes via voice mail through three degrees of separation, I admit I'm not always quick to return the call. But a few days later, Leah calls back. She's the one who tells me Charlie's story.

Down east in a little town called Benson, Charlie woke up in the middle of the night and smelled smoke. He stood up from the couch where he was sleeping, choking on smoke that was billowing down from the ceiling. He started to run out the front door, but he remembered Ms. Louise, the elderly woman who let him sleep on her couch. Her bedroom was through the kitchen. Charlie said he never felt the heat as he ran in to get her, as he dashed back through the kitchen, carrying her in his arms. He was standing with her out by the street, watching the little place go up in flames, when firefighters arrived and told him he should probably sit down. Next thing Charlie knew, he was waking up in a hospital ninety miles away. Two weeks had passed without him knowing it. Half of his body was covered in third-degree burns.

Despite all this, Charlie is improving. The social worker called because she's trying to help him think about where he will go when he's discharged in a week or so. Ms. Louise, who is in worse shape than Charlie, is being transferred to Texas, where her daughter lives. But Charlie, the homeless guy who was sleeping on her couch, now has no caring widow to go home to.

Nine times out of ten when we get a call like this, our rooms are already filled—often with people from our neighborhood who've eaten with us for years. As the years go by, it gets harder to meet a genuine stranger in Walltown. But every once in a while, when the social workers call, there's a space available after someone just moved out. Every once in a while someone calls to knock for Charlie and we send someone over to the hospital to say, "Come on in."

This time it's me who goes. I meet a man who is tall and wiry—half mummy, wrapped in gauze; half nervous energy, ready to jump off the curb. Charlie has in his possession four hospital-issue plastic bags. I help him put them in the trunk of the car. One has a few personal items—a toothbrush, a baseball cap, a change of clothes. The other three are packed full of medical supplies. I gather Charlie never had much in this world before the fire, but here's a man who really has lost everything, down to half of his skin.

Charlie is, like me, a white man from rural North Carolina.

On the car ride back to the house, I figure it's best to prepare him for our context. I tell him a bit of our story, emphasizing the way we've tried to live together across the dividing lines of race in a historically African American neighborhood. I tell him how I've found healing from the racism that I didn't know I had in me. I don't know Charlie, but I've known guys who look and talk like him. If it turns out that he's a card-carrying member of the Ku Klux Klan, I figure it's best for everyone if we can learn that on the ride home.

But Charlie tells me he started attending a black Baptist church when he was staying down in Benson. As a matter of fact, that's where he met Ms. Louise, a mother of that church who took him in and made him feel like family. He tells me how he loved to sit with her in her living room and sing gospel hymns that made her light up. She had become a mother to him, and he was glad to have the chance to get to care for her in her home. Her kids were living so far away, and she was beginning to need more help.

Earlier in the conversation, before I started trying to feel out Charlie's racial prejudices, I had tried in a sentence or two to explain what a hospitality house is and why we do what we do. But Charlie has already lived in a hospitality house. He is no stranger to the peculiar grace that draws us into the most unlikely of friendships—into this mysterious place where the guest becomes host in God's new family and the widow who takes in a wayfarer is saved from fire by the homeless guy on her couch. This, I remember, is why we do what we do. Because our guests often see more clearly than we can the grace by which all of us are saved.

———

Leslie is the daughter of Ms. Johnson, a woman at our church—a woman who lives one block down, who waves every time she passes the house and hugs us every Sunday at church. But also a woman with whom I've never had a serious conversation until she stops by to ask if her daughter can stay with us. Ray is living with us at the time. He has known Ms. Johnson all his life, and Leslie too. He tells us that Leslie has always been really quiet. She won't be any trouble.

Ms. Johnson, it turns out, is worried about her adult daughter not because she's hanging with the wrong crowd or bringing home babies for grandma to raise. Her concern is that Leslie is not interacting with anyone. Ms. Johnson wants to see her get out and get to know some people. Our house, she's noticed, is always bustling with people.

So Leslie moves in. She's quiet but very nice, always polite, and seems as focused as anyone has ever been on a goal. "I want to get a full-time, permanent job," she tells us. I tell her that sounds like a great idea.

We help Leslie move her things into a room upstairs. I walk past her room a couple of hours later, and she's sitting on the edge of her twin bed, reading from the Bible. I mention that we'll have dinner in a bit, and she smiles, saying thanks. But she doesn't come down for dinner. Someone goes up to tell her it's ready, and she says she'll come soon. But she doesn't.

Our rules for guests are few: You can't be active in addiction. You can't invite your boyfriend to move in. You can't be mean to others. Apart from these few basics, we try to communicate expectations that we all share as a community, inviting people into our shared life. So we expect everyone in the house to show up for dinner. It doesn't mean that you're put on some kind of probation if you miss three meals in a week. We're not running a shelter. We're more of an extended family. We want to love people toward health, not force them into a mold.

But we do, like any normal family, expect people to participate. So after Leslie skips dinner her first night and stays in her room until midmorning the next day, Leah goes up to talk to her. She asks if everything is all right, if she has plans for the day. "Oh yes," Leslie says. "I want to get a full-time, permanent job."

Over the next week, "full-time, permanent job" echoes in our house like the automated voice on my two-year-old's play kitchen. Attempts at conversation about what Leslie wants to do circle around this phrase, which she repeats with great earnestness. But she does not leave her room. We're not even sure when she slips into the bathroom. Every time anyone goes upstairs, Leslie is sitting on the edge of her bed, a Bible on her lap.

None of us is an expert in mental health, but it's obvious that something is wrong. Leslie is not just a shy young woman who needs to get out more. She's a terrified recluse, robotically repeating a goal for her future. What's more, when we describe to her what we've observed and ask her to make sense of it, she simply says again that she just wants to get a full-time, permanent job.

When every attempt to talk with Leslie has failed, I explain to her that we think she needs the sort of help that only a doctor can give her. We are happy to help her get that help. We add that if she is not willing to go to a hospital, she can't stay in this room. She says she has nowhere else to go; her mom won't let her come home. I start helping her pack her things. I'm not sure what to do, but I know Leslie can't stay here. She can't sit in this room forever. If nothing else, she'll die of starvation.

I decide to keep things simple. "It's time to leave," I say. "I can take you to the hospital, or I can take you to the homeless shelter." Leslie asks if she can use the phone to call a friend, and I say yes. She says this friend is glad for her to come stay with her.

When we arrive at the friend's apartment on the other side

of town, I go to the door. Leslie is hesitant about which door is her friend's. She doesn't move from the passenger's seat. I knock, but no one answers. I walk back to the car and ask Leslie if she knows where her friend might be, but she says nothing. She's staring out the windshield, her gaze fixed on the apartment building the same way it had been all week on the open Bible in her lap.

I start driving. Beside me is a woman who's scared to death, who cannot bring herself to move from whatever enclosure gives her a sense of security. I head toward the hospital. I know that she can't be admitted against her will, but I also suspect that if I can get her there—if I can get her seated in the waiting room—she'll be as glad to stay there as she has been to sit on the edge of a bed at Rutba House.

In John's gospel, when Jesus goes to the pool at Bethesda, he finds a fellow in one of the gazebos who can't move—a guy who's been lying there, waiting, for thirty-eight years. "Do you want to get well?" Jesus asks the man, suggesting that even Jesus can't heal someone against his will. The man's answer focuses on the injustice of his isolation: when the waters stir, he says, there's no one to help him get into the pool. But Jesus focuses on what the man can do with Jesus's help. "Get up! Pick up your mat and walk," Jesus says.

Leslie decides that she wants to be well. She stays at the hospital, starts taking medicine, and is discharged to a group home in Raleigh. Several months later, when I see Ms. Johnson at church, she's eager to talk. She has been to see Leslie at her new place. She's fat, Ms. Johnson says, by which she means that Leslie is eating, not wasting away in self-imposed seclusion. "Honey," Ms. Johnson says, "she's even got herself a full-time, permanent job."

Ms. Johnson lifts her hands above her head and twists them back and forth, just like all the church ladies do when they're praising the Lord. "I thank you, Jesus," she says with her eyes closed. I thank him too. It hasn't quite happened right in front of my eyes, but I've seen someone pick up their mat and walk. Here by the healing pool, one of God's children has been made well.

Eight

Voices in the Wilderness

I am standing in the kitchen, chopping onions at the counter, when Steven walks in and asks with his quiet but intense voice, "Do you have a sheet I can use?"

Steven has been here for about a week, and we're still trying to figure him out. When he showed up, unannounced, in our yard, he had a backpack slung over one shoulder. He might have been a student walking down from campus. But he told us he'd come from the interstate highway north of town, where a car stopped to offer him a ride. Thank you, he told the driver, but he preferred to walk. The Lord had called him to walk. He was wandering the land, trusting the Lord to provide for his needs.

"Well," this driver said to Steven, "when you get to Durham, you should go to the Rutba House. They'll probably let you stay the night with them." We did, and now Steven has been here a week. A quiet man, he's as young as the college student we first mistook him for, only his skin looks more like a sailor's, suntanned and rarely washed. He wears an unkempt beard.

It appears walking has been Steven's principle pastime for the past several months. When we ask where all he's been, he recounts a journey down the East Coast from Pennsylvania. He's done it all on foot, without an itinerary, trusting the good graces of whomever's path he crosses or spending a night under an overpass when no one welcomes him. He's learning to trust the Lord, Steven says. And he's learning to see America and Americans for who we really are.

This becoming a seer, it turns out, has prompted Steven's request for a sheet this afternoon. I ask what sort of sheet he's looking for, and he tells me he thinks the Lord is calling him to be a prophet. In the room at Rutba House where Steven has been staying, we have a shelf full of books on the Hebrew Bible. Maybe he's been reading up on Amos and Isaiah, Jeremiah and Elijah. "The Old Testament prophets had a uniform," he says. "They were recognizable as men of God. I, uh, need to make myself a robe. I mean…I think I need some kind of uniform if I'm going to walk the highway as a prophet."

I suggest that, as a young white fellow in this neighborhood, Steven might be careful about wearing a bedsheet and saying he speaks for God. Some folks might not appreciate the memories it calls to mind. Steven agrees, but he insists on his need for a distinctive garment. He seems to think it must be made from a sheet, so we settle on a baby-blue twin sheet. He cuts a hole for his head, trimming off one side to supply a strip of cloth that he ties around his waist for a belt. It's not quite camel's hair, but it's distinctive.

After morning prayer the next day, Steven says he's ready to hit the road. He has a word from the Lord to share with us before he goes. Looking a bit like a kid at his bar mitzvah holding the holy Scriptures for the first time, Steven is a little nervous. This is his first day wearing the mantle of a prophet. He clears his throat and begins to speak in his characteristic whisper.

"I have noticed in my travels that the automobile is a problem. It keeps people moving fast but at great cost. Our country is fighting a war for oil in the Middle East. Our roadsides are strewn with litter, beautiful countryside ruined by passing cars." I get the feeling that we're hearing the stump speech Steven has been working on since he left Pennsylvania on foot. But like any good preacher, he homes in on the particulars of our specific context. "I have noticed that the automobile is a problem here too. At your house meeting this week, you reported that the car co-op account was low after an unusual number of repairs. Just a few weeks ago, one of your members was struck by an SUV while she rode her bicycle. She was nearly killed by an automobile."

The prophecy has mounted to its climax, and Steven's eyes

are on fire. But he's still whispering. "What I hear the Lord saying is that you need to forsake the automobile and trust him." With this word, Steven decides his work in Walltown is done.

He asks for the best route to take out of town, then declines our hugs because of a vow he's made against human contact. He walks up the hill until he's just a small blue dot on the horizon, makes a left, and slips out of view. A couple of days later we get a letter from Steven. He stopped the first night out of Durham in a graveyard south of town, sleeping under the stars atop a crypt. His letter thanks us for our hospitality and reminds us that the automobile will be our demise if we don't turn from the destruction that is to come. The prophet signs off, his duty discharged, and we never hear from him again.

The trouble with prophets is that they almost always seem self-appointed, the established authorities being their chief targets. What's more, they never tell you what you'd like to hear. In a decade of trying to welcome the stranger, looking for that of God in each of them, we've had a few who stepped right out of the disguise of the stranger and claimed to be sent by God himself.

On Steven's departure, we do not dissolve the car co-op, sell our three vehicles, and commit to go only where our feet will take us. It doesn't seem that simple to us. But we have to admit there is some truth to what Steven has said. The day Leah calls to tell me that she and our daughter, Nora, have been broadsided at an intersection downtown, I remember Steven and his prophecy. No, we never want to hear what the prophet has to say, and it's no simple matter to figure out who speaks for God. But over time you learn to listen.

Maybe everyone who comes to the door isn't Jesus. But that doesn't mean they don't have something to teach you. Maybe they're another voice, crying out in the wilderness, "Prepare the way of the Lord."

Some prophets have a reputation that precedes them. We meet Marie through Isaiah House, a sister community across town— a hospitality house that welcomes mostly women and children. She is a woman in her sixties who has been making her way from hospitality house to hospitality house. Finding herself a middle-aged woman staying in a homeless shelter, Marie was overwhelmed by what it might take to become independent again. It wasn't that she didn't have the capacity to do what other Americans do. She had worked jobs, kept house, and raised a family with little help from the men in her life. But the odds stacked up against her, she lost everything, and she couldn't imagine how she would ever get back on her feet starting from zero. Landing in a shelter, Marie heard a call to serve the homeless as she lived among them.

Volunteering on a soup line in southeast Virginia, she met some people who called themselves Catholic Workers and said they lived in a hospitality house. They summed up for Marie the vision of their founder, Dorothy Day: Since Jesus promised to meet us in the homeless stranger, Catholic Workers keep Christ Rooms in their homes. They welcome anyone who needs a place to stay and work with them to build a new society within the shell of the old. Marie wasn't Catholic, but she was sure enough a worker. Dorothy Day spoke her language. Marie left the shelter and signed on for the Catholic Worker movement.

But she was still a Pentecostal in the way she practiced her faith. Every so often, God would speak to her in a dream, and she would know that it was time for her to get moving again. Marie learned to work the hospitality-house circuit, calling ahead to check where space was available. By the time she calls us, we've already met Marie several times. Her reputation precedes her: Marie is a woman who dives in and gets to work.

Her first day here, she deep cleans the kitchen, scrubbing crevices we didn't know we had. Marie embraces everyone she meets with a hearty hug and a "hallelujah." She is a woman for whom faith seems uncomplicated. God has called her to be about his business, so she's going to do it with a smile on her face and pep in her step. Clearly she has known suffering. But Marie has no time for doubt.

Still, I wonder how a woman like her gets cut off from everything she has known. Midway along the journey of her life she was homeless, and yet she just kept moving. I think about my grandmothers, both of them hard-working women like Marie from North Carolina's hill country. My grandmothers struggled to raise families in poverty, sometimes with little help from their men. With an unexpected illness or some other turn of bad luck, they might have ended up like Marie. But I can't imagine either one of them losing touch with their children. I can't imagine them just moving on.

When I get the chance, I ask Marie about her kids. She speaks lovingly of them as children, remembering the days when she took care of them at home. But she hasn't seen them in a long while. She isn't sure where some of them are. She pauses for a moment, and I think I see a tinge of grief in her eyes. But Marie is back to work in no time, singing a gospel tune as she sweeps floors. For some reason, she cannot stop. She has to keep moving.

When Marie tells us how much she loves the place—how she thinks this is the way people were made to live—we explain membership here and invite her to think about it. Maybe the Lord is calling her to keep serving others but to do it with a group of people who will take care of her also, in a place where she belongs.

Marie is getting older and knows she can't keep up this pace forever. She tells us she will pray about staying here.

I can see Marie making use of her great energy to wrestle with this decision. At morning prayer, as we sit facing one another across the circle in our living room, her face twists up and she is speaking in tongues, shouting down the demons in a language that God alone can understand. I'm not sure what all she's up against, but it's evident that Marie is in touch both with the basic spiritual issues of her life and with the God who is able to heal and restore.

Of course she is running from some of her shadows. Of course she needs to deal with her broken relationships. But in this moment of honest prayer, I can look around the circle and name ways that we all do, me included. I think of a quote that we have pinned on the bulletin board in our kitchen: "If you've come here to help me, you're wasting your time. But if you've come here because your liberation is bound up with mine, then let us work together."

This opening ourselves to one another has a mysterious power. Somehow, Marie's need exposes my own. Somehow, we are prepared to receive something new together. I say the same prayers I pray every morning, but today they taste like cold water on my thirsty tongue.

When Zeke nearly kills his wife, Trina, just hours after being released from jail, we are devastated but not surprised. Zeke is a big man with deep wounds. His mental illness went untreated for most of his life, and the crack he became addicted to as a teenager didn't help. Leah says Zeke is the only man she's ever been afraid of. Maybe I scare easier than she does. I'd add a few more to my list, but Zeke would be right there at the top.

We know Zeke because, back when we first moved here and Leah was still running the after-school program, he happened to be out of prison. At the free lunch that's served downtown seven days a week, Zeke met Trina. When they started flirting over the meat and three sides that day, he didn't know about Trina's six kids who were at school and day care. He went home with her and found himself in the midst of a chaotic family system. A few weeks later, when Zeke rammed Trina's car into another at an intersection, he made an emergency call to the Walltown Neighborhood Ministries. Drivers were dispatched to pick up Trina's children and bring them to Leah's after-school program.

This series of unlikely events is how we meet Zeke and Trina.

Somehow, in the midst of all the craziness, welcoming these six kids while managing thirty others, Leah sees what they're up against. She sees the desperate situation they have been born into, and it breaks her heart. Leah starts driving them home at the end of the day so they can keep coming to her after-school program. Sometimes she brings them to dinner at Rutba House so they can have a real meal before they go home. We get to know Zeke because Leah loves the kids of the woman Zeke happens to be with.

Zeke grew up in Walltown, around the corner from our house. His mother was ordained as an associate minister at Saint John's Baptist Church, where I serve on the pastoral staff. The old folks remember little Zeke, even though he's been locked up most of his adult life. He always was a troubled boy, they say.

For years we get a call every time Zeke goes off the handle. We pick up the kids and take them to their dad's. We visit Zeke in jail. We talk to Trina about their relationship. We listen as she cries, unable to imagine a way out of the cycle of abuse that keeps spiraling downward. One of the worst of many bad decisions we make over the years is to go with Zeke and Trina to the courthouse to witness their marriage. They need to be married so they can stay together in a homeless shelter for couples. We know almost as soon as we've done it that it was a mistake. Still, we feel all the more obligated to help them find some way out of the mess they're in.

Late one night, Trina calls. She's afraid Zeke is going to kill her. Leah and I drive to a motel on the edge of town and knock on the door of their room. Zeke tries to play it off. Everything is fine, he says. Trina's just a little worked up. I try to be firm without putting him on the defensive. We'd like to talk to her, I say.

Eventually, Trina comes out. But she has changed her tune. Yes, he was hitting her, but he's calmed down now. She's going to be okay. We tell her there's no need to risk it; she could get killed. She said it herself over the phone, just twenty minutes earlier.

But you can't make someone do what even they know is right. When Trina chooses to stay at the motel, I start to wonder if she'll make it out alive. Which is why we are devastated, but not surprised, the day we find out Trina is in the ICU. She is barely holding on to life, with nearly forty stab wounds all over her body. Zeke has been in jail for several months—long enough for Trina to meet another guy at the free lunch downtown. She invited him home.

Earlier in the same day when Trina winds up in the ICU, Zeke gets out of jail but does not call home. He runs into an old friend, and they get high together. By the time he walks in on Trina and her new boyfriend, he's already out of his head. When it's all over, he doesn't remember where he got hold of the butcher knife.

I know enough about prison that I cannot find it in myself to hope that anyone will be healed there. But I admit that I can't imagine anywhere else for Zeke. The psychologist who testifies at his trial says that someone with the borderline personality disorder he has can snap at any time, especially when under stress in intimate relationships. Zeke and Trina's marriage is not simply volatile; it is lethal. Prison bars, I figure, may be the only thing that can keep them alive.

But Zeke doesn't see it that way. He is angry at Trina, angry at the system, angry at himself, no doubt. What is more, he is angry at us. He writes from prison to tell us how he knows we were involved in his conviction and that we should be ashamed. Real Christians wouldn't treat a friend like that. We must have given in to Satan's temptation. We are the worst kind of traitors—wolves in sheep's clothing. Zeke quotes pages and pages of Scripture, warning us of the wrath that is to come.

I try to respond to his letters a time or two, but they just get worse. It is clear that Zeke's mental health has taken a nosedive. Maybe his confinement has saved Trina's life, but it looks to me like Zeke is gone. He lashes out at guards and attacks other inmates. He is transferred to solitary confinement at our state's only supermax facility. There he is cut off from all direct human contact. No fellow prisoners. No guards. No one. Just a cell, ten by six, with a fluorescent light shining down twenty-four hours a day.

Every once in a while, I send a note to tell him we are praying for him. He writes back, but his letters continue to pour out hate. I pray for him, but I am not sure what to ask God for.

"Have mercy," I whisper. I can't imagine what hope even looks like.

Then one day I get a letter from Zeke that is different. Jesus has met him in his cell, he says. Everything has changed. He is overwhelmed by joy.

I do not rise to shout hallelujahs. I sit at our kitchen table, rereading his words, unsure what to make of this change in tone. I'm skeptical because Zeke has always used (in my judgment, misused) spiritual language. What's more, I've seen a dozen jailhouse conversions that didn't stick. Who's to say this one is for real? I write a short note to celebrate Zeke's awakening of hope. But I also figure we'll have to wait and see.

Week after week, the letters keep coming. They seem honest. Sometimes they're even self-critical. But each one begins and ends, without fail, thanking God for his grace and mercy. I find myself eager to open the letters I used to avoid.

Leah decides to go online and check Zeke's infraction record with the Department of Corrections. It's a mile long, filled with citations for noncooperation, threats, assault against guards…up until the date when he wrote to say Jesus met him in his cell. After that, nothing. Not a single infraction.

We start to write more consistently. Zeke asks if we could pray at the same time every day, so we send him a copy of the prayer manual we use at the house and invite him to join us at 8 a.m. He says we can send our prayer requests to him in letters.

So we do. Zeke is still in supermax, but he's not alone. In some mysterious way, he's closer to us than he was when he lived in the neighborhood.

I am not eager to embrace this deepening of relationship with Zeke. As much as I've come to hate prison walls, I have to admit that I've trusted them too. Somehow I let myself believe that I was safer—that we were all better off somehow—with Zeke caged up like an animal. This is about more than my relationship with Zeke. It is, I suspect, tied up with the scores of people whose lives have become interwoven with ours over the past decade. I have lived, from the very beginning, with my eyes wide open looking for Jesus. I got into this because I wanted to be overwhelmed by the mysterious interruption of gifts from beyond. And I have been.

But that is not all. Deep down, I begin to realize, I have also been overwhelmed by the accumulated trauma of story after story, person after person. I have celebrated the interruptions of grace, but I have not taken the time to grieve the loss of kids who were molested before they had a chance to know what real love looks like. We talk, I have to admit, about community as a place where we learn to bear one another's burdens. But I have turned from the weight of these stories. I have, somehow, distanced myself from their pain. The cost, I see, is that my soul has become hard. I am experiencing a crisis of faith.

Of course, in the midst of the confusion, it is hard to name exactly what is going on. What I experience is moments when I find it hard to breathe. I can't eat, and my neck feels like I've been in a car crash. I slump into a chair and ask God for help. I try to pray, but I can't. I know I need help, but I'm not sure what kind or how to find it.

And then another letter from Zeke comes. He's been reading the Bible, and he wants to share what he thinks is a word from the Lord for me. It is a complicated reading of an obscure story from the history of Israel, the kind of passage you might skip over. But somehow Zeke is able to see in this story the way we humans harden our hearts in adversity and in so doing close ourselves off to the only thing that might save us. He is right This is exactly what I need to hear. Suddenly my struggle is clear. In this moment of clarity, tears streaming down my cheeks, I know that I can trust.

I don't think for one minute that it's a good thing that Zeke is in prison or that he nearly killed Trina or, for that matter, that I feel like I nearly drowned in despair trying to keep my head up and be strong as I faced powers far greater than me. I don't know why any of these things happened, and I would never have asked for it to be this way. But I do know that, here in the midst of the mess that we've made of this world, grace happens.

You wonder how many voices have cried out in the wilderness without anyone to hear them. But all you can say is "Thank you, thank you." Because, somehow, this one got through to you. A letter comes from the most unlikely prophet you can imagine, and you are saved.

Part 3

Gifts from Beyond

Nine

The Light That Can Shine

We make our decisions at Rutba House by consensus. At Monday-night meetings, week after week, we sit in a circle and listen to every voice, even the ones who repeat what they said last week. And the week before that. And the roughly 378 weeks before that.

After several years of doing this, we learn to delegate by consensus. Some decisions we can agree to entrust to one member or another: who will set up the budget or shop for groceries or meet with visitors to talk about what we're doing. Even still, some decisions require a conversation every time. Welcoming someone to live in our home is one of them. If everyone isn't "in," hospitality doesn't work.

On this particular Monday night, I am asking if a friend named Tim can come here for two years. He is a member of another community like ours, only theirs has been around a lot longer and has considerably more experience than we do. Tim is someone from whom I have learned, a man I respect who has lived in a hospitality house for nearly twenty years. His community has decided to send him to Durham to go to graduate school, but they would very much like him to be part of our community while he's here. This is a request not only from Tim but from all of them. Will we be a home away from home for this brother?

The prospect excites me, I admit, but I want to be a faithful messenger. I have a list of notes I jotted down during my phone conversation with Tim. He wants people here to know that he expects graduate school to be time consuming and that he knows himself well enough to anticipate that it will be difficult for him to be an active participant in our community. He also wants everyone to know he is gay.

Ray, who comes close to nodding off as I walk through this report, suddenly sits up and says, "Whoa, what's that? You say this guy is gay?"

I assure him that he heard right. Tim realized as a teenager that he was attracted to men, not to women. He tried to change this desire when he realized it wasn't shared by most of his peers. When that didn't work, he signed up for programs that tried to reorient his sexual orientation. But that didn't work either. So, for a while, Tim dated guys. He had a long-term, serious relationship with one man. But Tim decided that the intimacy he needs most is the fellowship of community and that his particular vocation in this context is to be single.

He is a single gay man who isn't looking for a relationship. He just wants everyone to know that this is part of who he is.

"Nope," Ray says, "I'm not living with him."

I ask Ray to explain his opposition. "I was in prison with a lot of those guys. I had to live with them. And I don't care what he says about not looking for a relationship. If you're gay, you're gay. And I ain't living with you."

This is an example of what we call blocking consensus. Ray is not expressing hesitancy or asking to hear another perspective from someone else. He is saying that he will not live with this man, case closed.

I tell Ray that he doesn't even know Tim, who is a personal friend. I mention that I am offended that Ray would write him off so easily. Ray says I'm right: he doesn't know Tim. It's nothing personal. He's just not going to live in the same house with a gay man.

Someone suggests that we all take time to think about it and talk again at our next meeting. This seems reasonable, but I can't imagine how anything might change.

Then someone asks Ray if he'd be willing to talk to Tim on the phone in the meantime. To me, this sounds like a terrible idea. What would these two talk about? I can imagine the awkward silence. What's worse, I cringe at the thought of Tim catching the brunt of Ray's antigay sentiment, which he holds on to from prison. Such a conversation could not possibly end well.

But Ray agrees. He'll call Tim. Hesitantly, I give him the number. At our next meeting, Ray reports that he has talked to Tim—they had a real heart-to-heart—and Tim answered all his questions. Has Ray changed his mind? "No, I still don't want to live with a gay man." But he concedes, "If y'all want him to come and live in the other house, I'm not going to stop it."

A few months later, Tim moves in. As we do every year about this time, the whole Rutba House crew piles into a few cars and drives west a couple of hours for a retreat in the mountains. We listen to one another's stories, take hikes together, and sit up late singing songs and playing board games. It's a time to be together, to welcome new people into our family, and to recommit to our covenant for shared life as a community. This time of commitment takes place in a service that we pull together at the end of the weekend. Before we read our covenant aloud, there's a time for people to say anything they want the whole community to hear.

Ray knows how this goes. And as it happens, he is sitting beside Tim in our circle. "I've got something I need to say," he asserts, shifting forward to the edge of his seat. "Now, y'all know I wasn't excited about Tim here coming. He knows it too." I'm not sure where Ray is going with this, but I can tell he's earnest, choosing his words carefully.

I watch as he reaches out and puts his hand on Tim's knee. "I just want to say, you all right, man."

Both men laugh, and the rest of us are laughing with them, glad to release the tension that has been building since that first house meeting months ago. I do not anticipate that Ray and Tim will go on to become friends, that when Tim's two years here are through that Ray will be the first one to get on a plane to go visit him. But watching these two laugh, I glimpse a light shining out of their lives.

Their laughter is a light on a lamp stand.

You don't see this every day. It's not as if people walk around here glowing. But maybe because you've spent so many nights stumbling in the darkness, your eye is sensitive to the light. You know without a second thought that this is what you were made for.

In her elegant poem "Singapore," Mary Oliver recalls an encounter with a poor woman who is cleaning an ashtray in a toilet bowl in an airport restroom. Oliver is both repulsed by the thought that this is the woman's daily work and struck by the simple beauty with which the woman uses a blue rag to polish the ashtray. How when she looks up, embarrassed, her smile is "only for my sake." The poet longs to see this woman rise up from her base existence—to soar like the bird she was made to be, like the bird that she is. But then she reflects that she is not asking for anything miraculous. She only means "the light that can shine out of a life."

Leaning into the darkness and listening to people who have suffered the worst that our society has to offer, you learn what Oliver is getting at. Something deep in each of us cries out against the injustice of poverty and homelessness, of prison and addiction. This repulsion is visceral when we confront any one of these realities not as an issue but as the pain at the heart of a friend's life. Statistics about the overwhelming numbers of people who live and die in poverty and pain are sobering. But numbers can also depersonalize the suffering of people we don't know but still care about. The hard facts somehow distance us from the emotion of a human life.

But one person unveils the fullness of our pain and our hope. One relationship can help us see the light that can shine out of a life—the very thing that, though it isn't a miracle, really, illuminates the way home for each of us.

⁂

When Debbie calls to tell us about David, she has to first tell me who she is. These are the days before caller ID, and I didn't recognize her voice. Debbie is from Jewish Family Services, and she is curious if Rutba House might be able to help David. His is, she admits, a peculiar case.

Debbie met David several months ago when he came by her office with a couple seeking assistance. They were new to the area and not part of one of the local synagogues. They were caring for this elderly gentleman, David, and they were struggling to find work. They needed a little help with paying the bills. Debbie helped them, and each time they came back, their story wore a bit thinner. Debbie began to suspect that the couple was playing the charity game—another town, another story. She'd seen it enough times to know that the minute she called their bluff, they'd be gone.

But David beat her to it. He stumbled into the office one afternoon, wheezing and out of breath. Debbie helped him to a chair and listened as David confirmed her suspicions—the couple was, indeed, a team of professional charlatans. What's more, they had kidnapped David, seeing his monthly SSI check as a potential income stream. When he objected, they told him it was in his best interest. When he tried to resist, they beat him up and locked him in a room.

David made it to Debbie's office by escaping the apartment while his captors were out. He ran to the only place he could remember how to get to. Bewildered, he told Debbie that he couldn't believe he let himself be taken in like that. He had begun to wonder if he would ever make it out alive.

Since that meeting, Debbie has been putting David up in a hotel across town. But she is reaching far outside her normal circles—beyond any reference she's given this couple—to keep David safe from them. I invite the two of them to join us for dinner, and we meet the rail-thin, white-haired man who has survived this terrible story. He has a smoker's cough and a dry sense of humor.

David is a likable fellow, and his immediate need is evident. We're a house for people like him. But the decision about whether to invite David to come isn't an easy one. We have room enough, yes, but part of the reason a bed remains vacant is that everyone here feels overextended, worn out by a steady stream of other people's needs on top of an intense season of work for all of us.

We've been hosting people—one, two, three at a time—for several years. We have experience, but that does not make opening your life any easier. I start to think experience may even make it harder. Sure, you know the story about Ray and Tim becoming friends. You know dozens of stories, not only about people becoming well, but also about how guests have helped you heal, pushed you to grow into the person you were made to be. You know the stories, but you are not naive about their cost. Saying yes to David is a yes to the light that can shine out of a life. But it's also a yes to the mess that he finds himself in.

So, what to do? Like prayer, the process of discernment is a mystery. By what calculus do you measure the costs and benefits of another human life? I've listened to people considering marriage, to couples who are thinking about having kids. We all try to figure this out at one time or another. But our familial relationships depend upon the fact that they are almost never the result of calculated decisions. We fall in love, or we fall into bed. No one thinks about the years of dirty diapers. Our fragile human existence depends on people remaining true to commitments we make not because they are the smart thing to do, but because we long for another—because we cannot, in the moment at least, imagine doing anything else.

What, then, binds together this peculiar family—this community—that is not born of passion or blind love? It is not easy to pin down. We sit in a circle, listening to one more story that is too often like the stories we've heard before. Communities have their limits, and we have learned to be honest about ours. But the mystery to me is in seeing how the yes comes, how a group of people can choose to open themselves to the light, even when we are stumbling in the dark.

These yeses, I realize, are what make us into a community. We say yes not once and for all, but to David at this moment. We say yes to the light that can shine out of one life. We say yes together, as if holding hands in the night, and step out into the unknown.

When David moves in, he assumes a position on the couch by our front door, where he sits ten to twelve hours a day with a cup of tea and a Bible. He's never really read the Bible, he tells us. He decides to start at the beginning and read straight through. What's more, he is always eager to hear how you're doing when you come in the door, always glad to tell you about the most fascinating story that he was just reading. "Did you ever hear this one?"

When I was growing up, my great-granny lived with us. She was always there when I got home from school, always eager to listen. As I sat and ate her biscuits, warm out of the oven, she told me stories about growing up in the hills of southern Virginia, fetching milk from the spring box and carrying chickens down the main road to trade them at market. When you're eight years old, the great wide world of school can feel like a wild and crazy place some days. Coming home to Granny's stories and biscuits was a stabilizing rhythm, I realize. Maybe my parents thought we were caring for Granny. Maybe we were. But to me, her presence was an anchor in the storms of my early life.

David and my granny came from different worlds, but they are alike in this way: they have time to be present. This world where police officers raid houses with concussion grenades and friends are snatched off the streets without notice can often feel as crazy as an elementary school is to an eight-year-old. But here is David, keeping vigil by the door with a steady smile and a listening ear. For this struggling little community, he becomes an anchor.

In a rule of life that became the bedrock of Western monasticism, the sixth-century saint Benedict of Nursia wrote this simple and practical instruction:

> By the door of the community, place a sensible older
> member who has basic secretarial skills and is glad to sit
> and welcome people. This member will need a room
> close to the entrance so that visitors will always find him
> there to answer them. As soon as anyone comes knock-
> ing or asking for help, he should say, "Praise the Lord,"
> or, "Blessings," as he answers the door promptly with all
> the warmth of God's love. If he needs help with this
> job, the doorkeeper should be assigned a younger
> member as an assistant.

As far as I know, David has never read these instructions. His secretarial skills are somewhat questionable. He often has a story about someone who came by but can't remember their name or exactly what they wanted. Still, David keeps Benedict's ancient rule more closely than some of us who've tried to reshape our lives around it. He's not just a good guest. He has also become our host, keeping vigil by the door, practicing the kind of radical hospitality that first inspired us to come here.

Some of the guys from the street realize that this Jewish grandfather is willing to listen to their woes without judgment, willing to bear their troubles without trying to fix them. He is not put off by their crude language. He simply greets them as they are with the blessing of his presence and a smile that is for their sake. Every once in a while, he chimes in with a story of his own. I notice that a circle of these twenty-something guys is almost always gathered around David when I come home.

After a few months, David finishes his survey of the Bible, all conducted from the same spot on our living-room couch, punctuated by community prayers and dozens of rap sessions with young guys from the neighborhood. Undeterred by the interruptions, David has obviously been captivated by his reading. I ask what sense he makes of it all. "Well, I'm a Jew," he says. "But Jesus was a Jew too. I don't see any reason why I shouldn't be a Jew and a Christian. But I'm not going to be one of these Bible-thumping Christians. I want to love people—to live like Jesus lived."

I think of John's gospel—that story of Jesus's life that begins like the Jewish Torah with the words "In the beginning." Since the foundation of the world—since the beginning of all things—John says that the logic of the universe was a Person and that his "life was the light of all" people. Wherever there is life, this light shines on. Even in the deepest darkness. John says nothing has ever overcome this light.

If Jesus showed us what it looks like for this light to shine out of human flesh, he also invites us to see that it's there beneath our skin—that we kindle the flame when we embrace it, especially in those who have been forgotten and pushed aside. The light that is in each of us can shine out. It illuminates the person across from you so that you see them, often as if for the first time. With your eyes wide open, you don't only see the child of God across from you; you also reflect their light back to them. By the light that shines out of each of us, we learn to see each other.

This opening your life to Jesus isn't so much about finding the light in the stranger at the door as it is about watching a peculiar community catch fire, the light in each person shining more brightly as we receive the gift of another. Four months ago, we weren't sure we had it in us to welcome David. We weren't sure we could bear the load of one more person. But as David prepares to move into the subsidized senior housing that we helped him apply for, we're not sure how we might go on without him.

Maybe Benedict was right. Maybe we don't only need an older member by the door to welcome visitors. Maybe we also need a younger person by his side, apprenticing himself to the grandfather's practice of hospitality. When David is gone, I realize that I have been that apprentice. David has been my teacher in a school I didn't expect, inviting me to see the light that shines brighter than any darkness.

When you are engulfed in flames—when this light is bursting forth from the lives around you—it is strange how clouded in smoke it all seems. Like the three ancient Hebrew children tossed into Nebuchadnezzar's fiery furnace, you hear about it after the fact from an observer who tells you what she saw. To you, it seems like a blur. But to her, it looked like there was a fourth person walking with you in the flames. This sight touched something deep inside her, she tells you. Some primal force pushes her from a darkness she can't quite name toward this luminous mystery. She wonders how she might draw closer, how she might herself catch flame.

Such a person starts visiting us at Rutba House. After meeting her twenty or thirty times, we set up an internship for Lynn. The term *internship* misleads when it suggests this might be good preparation for some future job. We weed those people out. But we invite others to do this because they keep asking, because this way of life turns out to be a good deal of work and we find that we often need extra hands. Just one or two people at a time. As with everything here, the internship takes shape around the lives of those who come to do it.

A few years into this, a young man who just finished pre-med at an Ivy League school helps me see what our internship is for. "I've been in school all my life," he says. "And I'm going to be in school for several more years. I know what it takes to become a doctor. But before I do any more school, I need to learn how to live." I guess that's what we're all here for—to learn how to live.

To keep things simple, especially for young people who have been in scheduled programs all their lives, we make the internship a yearlong experience. It starts in September, like most schools, and ends the following summer. We plan a time in the spring to talk with our interns about what the next step is for them. Often it's the first time they've had a group of people with whom to discern this sort of thing.

By the time spring comes around, we know that it has been a difficult year for Lynn. She was a psych major in college and went abroad with a missions group for several months before coming here. Listening to her, we begin to see that she studied psychology to try to make some sense of the familial confusion she grew up in. Her year spent halfway around the world was probably driven by a need to get away from all of this. But her time here, it seems, is when everything comes crashing down on Lynn and her family. Her parents separate and file for divorce. The boyfriend she thought she would marry decides to move on.

In the living room where she has sat every morning for prayer and has been part of Monday-evening community meetings—in this circle that has become familiar—Lynn tells us she can't see a way forward. Everything she assumed would be there has fallen apart. It is as if the ground has opened up and swallowed her. Only, she observes, life here feels stable. Somehow, the daily rhythm makes sense. This odd family of adopted sisters and brothers who share a table has become for her the truest home she knows. She asks if she might stay another year. We tell her she might need more time, but yes, of course. She's welcome.

This young woman, bright and beautiful, came here to serve—to welcome the homeless, to live among the poor. And she has. But her housemates and neighbors also have helped her come to a place where she is not ashamed of her pain, of her neediness. Their need—our need—has put her in touch with her own. She asks for help, and some of those whom she came to serve wrap their arms around her and whisper, "It's gonna be all right, baby." Lynn cries and cries. And while the tears are still glistening on her cheeks, her face lights up with a smile.

A few weeks later, walking home from a service at church, I notice Lynn talking to a young man who has been around the church for a while, a guy I like a great deal. He doesn't know all that's been going on in Lynn's life, but there is a brightness in her presence that catches his eye—something he hadn't noticed before. He too is drawn to this light.

A year later these two are married at our church. When the service is over, we all walk down Onslow Street to the neighborhood recreation center and party all afternoon. The decorations, the food, the games for neighborhood kids—everything is a labor of love, homemade by this multiracial extended family of the formerly homeless and those of us who have found that our home is with them. This life, you know, is shot through with pain too deep for words. But it also is filled with an unspeakable joy. It is punctuated with parties, large and small. Even though you know you can't dance, you grab the hand of a kid you've known since her momma left her at grandma's house on her way to prison, and both of you laugh until the music is over.

A couple of years later, walking down Onslow Street, I stop to talk to Ms. Robinson, who is sitting on her porch. She has lived here all her life, and she has borne the pain of this place in her body. We sat and cried together when her son went to jail, and I observed the mixture of fear and anger on her face the day after bullets were sprayed into her house by a drive-by gunman. We also talk about flowers while her grandkids play with my kids. With a little time to spare this evening, I stop to catch up.

"You know," Ms. Robinson says with some enthusiasm, "Lynn asked me to come and talk to her girls on Wednesdays." I've heard this from Lynn, who coaches a team of girls in our after-school program for middle school kids from the neighborhood. But I'm interested to hear what it has been like for Ms. Robinson. "Oh, I just love it," she says. "I love talking to those girls. But I love to listen to Lynn too. She's something special." Ms. Robinson is right.

A light shines in the darkness, and the darkness has not overcome it.

Ten

Fire in My Bones

At our weekly potluck meal we meet Elizabeth, a young white professional who has purchased a rehabbed house in Walltown. Elizabeth has been to a few neighborhood association meetings. She is eager to know what's happening and ready to get involved. She works at the university, frequently travels internationally, has an eight-month-old daughter, and says she is interested in starting a neighborhood watch. Elizabeth is a woman of considerable energy. I wonder when she sleeps.

Regarding her idea about a neighborhood watch, I say in passing—trying to be direct but not confrontational—"No need to worry about a neighborhood watch. There's a grandma keeping watch on every block in this neighborhood. Get to know her, and you'll know what's going on." I notice that Elizabeth doesn't laugh. This should be a sign to me. Humorless white people with extra energy can be dangerous.

On leaving, Elizabeth thanks us for our hospitality (by

which she means our cordial conversation over dinner) and says to everyone in the room, "My house is just three blocks down on the left. Stop by any time." This is during a summer when Ant is home from college. One evening when he's walking to the park to play basketball, he remembers Elizabeth's invitation. Ant knocks on her door, meets Elizabeth's husband and daughter, has a glass of lemonade, and makes small talk. Somewhere in the course of the conversation, the neighborhood watch idea comes up again.

"As somebody who grew up here," Ant says, "I'd say you might want to be careful how loud you talk about that idea. There's some guys who might throw a rock through your window if they hear you're snitching to the police."

Ant says this without an agenda, other than to gently help a newcomer see that she is white—that she is an outsider. In Walltown, she is suspect simply because of the color of her skin.

The following afternoon I answer a knock at the door and see a police officer standing there. He explains that he's not here with a warrant and that it's not clear to him that anyone has done anything wrong. But he wants me to know that a woman down the street reported that a young man from our house had spoken to her in a way that she interpreted as a threat. As the officer is telling me this, I am not aware of Ant's visit the day before with the new neighbor. This conversation with a police officer comes as a surprise.

But I realize what has happened: a young white woman talked to a young black man, and when his words scared her, she called the police. I thank the officer for his caution in pursuing the complaint and assure him that, whatever misunderstanding occurred, it must have been just that—a misunderstanding. I've known Ant for years, I tell him, and I'm certain he would not threaten or seek to intimidate a neighbor. I tell him that Ant is here on break from college, working with kids from the neighborhood in a summer camp at our church. My head is spinning, but I try to act nonchalant. I lay on my thickest southern drawl with this white middle-aged police officer. On his way out the door, we chat about the weather.

But as soon as he is gone, I shift gears. My hands are trembling. I am angry in a cold and aching way, in that way that makes it possible to be mad and scared at the same time. I need to act fast. Ant is working at the summer camp, but he needs to know the police are coming, that a white man in a blue uniform is about to accuse him of threatening a white woman. (In Oxford, North Carolina, where Ant's family is from, a black Vietnam veteran named Henry Marrow, a peer of Ant's mother, was shot dead in the street by a white man in 1970. The white man testified in court that Marrow had spoken inappropriately to his daughter-in-law; the shooter was acquitted by an all-white jury.)

Of course, Ant knows this. He has grown up under the controlling gaze of suspicious eyes. He knows this is a reality that must be negotiated if he is to survive. But Elizabeth does not know this. She does not realize that her ignorance is a danger to everyone in this neighborhood. I call Ant's cell phone to give him a heads-up.

Then I send Elizabeth an e-mail to ask if we can plan a time for her to talk with us about what happened. She replies, saying she does not feel safe coming to our house alone. She would like to bring along representatives from the Partners Against Crime (PAC) group that she's been talking to about a neighborhood watch. We agree and plan a time to meet, but when the evening comes, there is no Elizabeth. Instead, Leah and I are sitting in our living room with Ant, another Rutba House member, and two middle-aged white people we've never met before.

We take a few minutes to get to know our guests, but the situation feels odd—talking to people we don't know about something that happened between Ant and a neighbor who's not here to participate. I decide the best we can do is try to help these two delegates see why race matters in our neighborhood, why the young white woman who just moved here shouldn't start a "watch" to help the police round up her neighbors before she even knows their names. As a white guy myself, I figure it might help to tell my story, to say something about how friends like Ant have helped me learn that I was a racist without even knowing it.

I try this approach, but it fails to achieve the desired effect.

The problem is not race, this man and woman explain. The problem is crime. They each have personal stories about how, years ago, someone broke into their homes and forever changed their view of the world, even the course of their lives. I do not bother telling them that the people who have robbed us did not have to break in. I know from experience how violating it feels, how the experience of being robbed creates fears that were not there before. But I try to explain how, in the particular case we're talking about, it was not Elizabeth's property that was endangered, but Ant's life.

Ant tells the visitors how it feels to be invited in to chat over lemonade about the neighborhood only to find out from a police officer the next day that his host "felt threatened." He explains in respectful but no uncertain terms that he has no desire to talk to the visitors about his neighbor. He wanted to talk to her and is frustrated that she sent representatives to answer for her. I watch him pour his heart out—I see the tears welling up in his eyes—and I am moved by Ant's capacity for restraint.

But the earnest souls who came to talk about the virtues of a neighborhood watch can't see Ant. They are blind. The white gentleman with a French-style moustache tells stories about how he works with white, black, and brown folks to make their neighborhoods safer. He loves eating fried chicken and watermelon at PAC block parties. Some of his best friends are black, he says with a smile. I am not making this up.

Our female guest is more clearly frustrated. She feels accused. She is a victim of crime, not a perpetrator. How dare we accuse her of racism? "My family never owned slaves," she says.

It is after midnight, and we have been talking for nearly four hours. I believe in dialogue, but I can't take this anymore. I stand up, open the door, and ask our guests to leave. Thrown off by my awkward interruption of our constant back and forth, Mr. Moustache attempts to sum things up—to name the ground that we've covered. But I cut him off. "I'm sorry," I say, "it's time to go now."

I tense up thinking about it, even now. In a decade of welcoming everyone, looking for the gift in every guest, these two visitors are the only people I have asked to leave my home.

After a week or so, after I have told this story a couple dozen times, I realize that those two people whose stubborn ignorance seemed so outrageous are not unlike me. They could well be my aunt and uncle—or my cousins who were raised right here in Durham on the north side of town. If I were on a flight to Chicago and these two sat beside me, we would surely find an hour's worth of things to talk about—things we share in common. In another setting, I might even enjoy the conversation.

But something has happened to me and to others here at

Rutba House. Welcoming the homeless has exposed my inner demons and convinced me of love's ultimate power, despite its steep costs. Knowing people here has taught me to see the world differently.

The stories have shaped what I see and how I see it.

Israel's ancient prophets, with their unkempt beards and wild eyes, were called seers for a reason. They saw what others could not—or would not—see, often because they relocated themselves. They chose to reside among the rejected and marginalized of their society. Jeremiah, a giant among the seers, said a time came when he could no longer keep quiet—when his message was like "fire shut up in my bones," burning to burst out and be heard.

No wonder the prophets could be harsh.

I recall Dr. Martin Luther King Jr. writing from a Birmingham jail cell, trying to explain to his white fellow ministers why he could no longer wait for change to come gradually. For the first time it occurs to me that King was a prophet not because he heard voices or dreamed dreams but because of what he had seen:

> When you have seen vicious mobs lynch your mothers
> and fathers at will and drown your sisters and brothers
> at whim, when you have seen hate-filled policemen
> curse, kick, brutalize, and even kill your black brothers

and sisters with impunity, when you see the vast majority of your twenty million Negro brothers smothering in
an air-tight cage of poverty in the midst of an affluent
society...then you will understand why we find it
difficult to wait.

I was not living in Birmingham in 1964, but I know that
the disparity between the median income of whites and African Americans in the South has not changed since then. Not at
all. I have gotten out of bed at 4 a.m. to carry breakfast to the
guys on the labor line. In the dark before dawn, I have seen the
sons of sharecroppers waiting their turn to do backbreaking
work for minimum wage. I have watched their sons and daughters, tempted to make an easy dollar, catch their first felony
charge for drug possession. I have seen them come home from
prison and apply for dozens of jobs, only to get one that's a
ninety-minute bus ride across town. Bus fare adds up, and they
are making only $7.50 an hour. The retail clerks are required to
wear the khaki pants and collared shirt that the store sells, and
so they find themselves, like their grandparents before them, in
debt to the company store.

When one of the children of the men in the labor line,
through years of hard work and the gift of a sharp mind, goes
to college and lands a steady job, you celebrate of course. You
scrape together every dime you have, rent out his favorite

restaurant, and invite everyone he knows to come and feast the day he walks across a stage to receive his degree, with honors. And when the white lady who moved in up the street calls the cops on him, then sends her friends from the neighborhood watch to deal with it, you learn what the prophet was talking about when he wrote about fire shut up in his bones. You feel the fire.

If you give a man a fish, the proverb says, he'll eat for a day. But if you teach him to fish, he'll eat for a lifetime. It's true enough, I suppose, if the problem is that people don't know how to fish. But if the problem is that, for generations, some people have sent others to do their fishing for them but refused to pay for the fish because they say they own the pond, then teaching a man to fish is not just patronizing. It's a slap in the face.

The old proverb is right about this much: feeding people at your dinner table is not a strategy to end hunger, just as welcoming guests as if they are Christ is not a way to end homelessness. But you are not here to fix a problem called homelessness. You are here to open yourself to a mystery you do not understand. You are here to learn through friendship what it might mean not to try to help people but to struggle with them for the justice that lifts us all.

After Mac has been part of Rutba House for a couple of years, I read a story in the newspaper about a local homeless shelter's expansion plans. I remember that Mac stayed at this place once—that he ran its kitchen before he joined Rutba House. "They're putting on another wing over there," I tell him, and he shakes his head and smiles. "They already own a city block," he says, "all paid for by people who feel sorry for a poor man like me."

Mac tells a story about how one winter night, when it was extra cold outside, a news crew for a local TV station came by to film people coming in off the streets. Only their timing was off. No one had come in yet. So someone handed Mac a blanket and told him to lie down on the floor in the corner so the cameraman could catch the desperate situation. Mac just laughed and walked away, saying he wasn't there to audition for a play. But someone else agreed to do it. "We had so many turkeys come in the next day we filled up a walk-in freezer," Mac recalls.

Having worked hard all his life, Mac knows the value of labor. He doesn't have a degree in economics, but he can add up in his head the total cost of a shelter that runs on donations. He doesn't need a spreadsheet to see that the majority of the money goes to paid staff who are there to manage "clients," while the cooking, cleaning, maintenance, and income-earning work is done by people like him. In return for their labor, residents get "three hots and a cot," which is, incidentally, the same thing they can get at the county jail for doing nothing.

The advantage of the shelter, you might say, is that you're at least free to come and go as you please. But Mac found that this wasn't always the case. When he put in a request to go to church on Sunday—to catch the bus and worship at our church, where he was already a member—the staff of this religiously supported shelter informed him that our church was not on the approved list. When he asked to see the list of churches that were approved for residents of the shelter, he was given the names of three overwhelmingly white, conservative Baptist churches. When Mac asked what was wrong with his church, he got a thirty-minute lecture on Christian doctrine.

Mac is no more a theologian than he is an economist, but it didn't take him two minutes to figure that his momma had known Jesus far better than this white man did. He walked out on the doctrine lesson and left his bed at the shelter with it. This, I learn, is how Mac first came to live in the apartment across the street from our house.

You don't read these stories in the paper; you don't hear them when you volunteer to serve on the soup line. But reading the morning newspaper with Mac, you get a lesson about the homeless industry—how it works and whom it benefits. Fifteen years ago, when I thought my life's work was to get to the White House for Jesus, I went to work for the senior senator from Mac's home state of South Carolina. This man once ran for president as a Dixiecrat, vowing to resist the freedom movement that said people such as Mac's parents had a right to vote. I recall the only advice Senator Strom Thurmond ever gave me: "Be careful, son. This is a dangerous town." He meant that it was important to avoid the homeless man who would stop a person in his tracks—the hunched-over African American man who would force a person to rethink his whole life without ever saying a word.

But it was a homeless man outside Union Station who interrupted me. At first, I thought the point of the interruption was that politics wasn't the answer. Jesus was the answer. So I changed direction and devoted my life to Jesus.

This is not my story; it is the story of a community of people. There are many who have lived and worked at Rutba House for varying lengths of time. After listening to stories such as Mac's and letting the stories get down in your bones, you know with everything in you that Jesus is the answer. And you know, just as surely, that Jesus is calling you deeper into God's politics of justice and peace.

But that is not all. You have not simply figured out how to marry your personal piety to a political vision, as important as that might be. No, this life in a hospitality house has been an invitation into the struggle that is your salvation. You might have worked all your life to achieve a level of power where you could legislate righteousness from the most prominent city on the planet. But you know now that if you had made it to the White House, it would have cost you your soul. It would have kept you from the relationships that have taught you what trust means, why companionship is essential, how love does its slow and mysterious work on those who open themselves to it.

At a retreat with a veteran from the Civil Rights movement, I learn a song that folks started singing in the late 1960s, when the movement seemed to be coming apart:

We are building up a new world,
We are building up a new world,
We are building up a new world,
Builders must be strong.

This strength to keep on building—to keep imagining the community that is yet to appear, despite the forces that say change is impossible—does not come from the inner resolve that I tried to cultivate as an ambitious teenager. No, this strength comes from learning the stories of those who have gone before—the abolitionists who worked forty years to do away with a system whose end they knew they would not see before they died. Still they worked, many of them vowing to live in their homes as if slavery had already been abolished, whatever the cost. Those hospitality houses became known as the Underground Railroad. They were America's first Civil Rights movement.

One hundred fifty years later, young people from the Student Nonviolent Coordinating Committee set up Freedom Houses in rural Mississippi—white and black together working to educate and organize poor black communities. They were tapping into the strength that comes from joining people in their struggle and inheriting the faith that can only be received there, at Canaan's edge. "God can make a way out of no way," the old folks said. They were talking about Israel in Egypt. They were talking about the freedom movement in rural Mississippi. They were talking about a power that is greater than our fears. They knew they had found something worthy of their lives.

This strength to build a new world is itself a gift. It comes to us from beyond, from the spring that is the source of every living thing. And it comes to us through people who know down in their bones that the world is not as it was made to be.

Somehow the fire that stirs in them sets you and me aflame, and we are, together, like the bush that Moses saw in the wilderness—burning, but not consumed.

We are becoming an eternal flame.

Second Coming

At Saint John's Missionary Baptist Church, we sing a song
that is charged with all the anticipation that expectant mothers
feel in their third trimester, that a man who has spent twenty
years behind bars experiences the night before his meeting with
the parole board:

> I wanna be ready,
> I wanna be ready,
> I wanna be ready
> to walk in Jerusalem just like John.

The John who is referenced here is the author of the New
Testament's Apocalypse—the John who, while a prisoner on
the island of Patmos, saw Jerusalem descending from the heavens and heard a voice telling him to pay attention and write it all
down. This John is, according to tradition, the same John who

wrote an account of Jesus's life—the Saint John for whom our church is named. He is the only one of Jesus's twelve disciples who was not martyred for his faith, the lone friend who was left to wait, to anticipate the coming again of the Jesus he had loved.

Along with John, you want to be ready when Jesus comes—when the trumpet sounds and the heavens break open and the dead rise from their graves to walk again. It is, indeed, a great and terrible expectancy.

"This being human is a guest house," Rumi says, and you have learned that it is true. The knock comes whether you want it to or not. It is always an interruption. Ten thousand hours of practice do not make you a master of receiving gifts from beyond. If anything, you know how often you have failed.

But you want to be ready, just like John, because there is, always it seems, a second coming. The knock that you ignore at midnight comes again when you're eating breakfast. By a grace that you don't entirely understand, you open the door and welcome a life you could never have planned.

Dostoevsky was right. "Love in action is a harsh and dreadful thing compared with love in dreams." You are not hoping for a utopia to suddenly appear in the sweet by-and-by. You are not waiting for Jesus to come whip everybody into shape once and for all.

No, you are learning that Jesus is risen and that he's coming again. He's coming for supper tonight, and he's not alone. Jesus is bringing with him Ms. Lewis and Ray, Quinton and Greg, Gary and Ant, Marie and Steven. He's standing at your door with someone whose name you don't yet know. They are sitting now at your dinner table—a peculiar family, for sure—ready to pass the butter and tell you a story about what happened today.

These stories are not finished. Our healing is not complete. Justice has not come flowing down like waters, nor righteousness like an ever-flowing stream.

But this future that you hope and pray for—this longing that burns so hot it keeps you up at night—has intruded upon your present. As messy and painful as it is, you know that the only solution is love. You keep believing because love keeps knocking, keeps coming to you in the flesh of this family that eats together.

In the midst of his apocalyptic vision, John heard Jesus say, "I stand at the door and knock. If anyone hears my voice and opens the door, I will come in and eat with that person, and they with me."

Heaven is a banquet, you know, not only because John saw it two thousand years ago but also because you see it at your dinner table. The knock comes once again, and you open the door to see who's there.

You do not know what tomorrow will bring, but you whisper the only grace that makes sense at such a meal: "Thank you. Help us. Come, Lord Jesus. Amen."

Acknowledgments

A politician knows to acknowledge the important people in the room before he begins his speech. But I know the acknowledgments can come only at the end of a book. If you have read this far, you know how indebted I am to the host of friends I've shared life with at Rutba House—the people whose stories I've tried to tell.

A note about these friends: they never asked me to write about them, and I don't believe my desire to tell their stories ought to further complicate their lives. So while the stories I have told here are, to the best of my knowledge, true, I have changed names and occasional identifying details to protect the privacy of friends.

This book would not have been possible without the trust that scores of people have extended me over the past ten years in Walltown. I have told these stories from my own perspective, paying attention to the ways they have shaped me. But this way of telling them may not make clear enough how much my relationships here depend upon the hard work of my fellow community members. Without them, there would be no Rutba House.

But even a community is not an island unto itself. I have Phyllis Tickle to thank for pointing out to me, with the clarity that she always possesses, how these stories do not reveal the degree to which our life at Rutba House depends upon a broad network of hospitality houses, intentional communities, churches, and families that pray for us, work with us, and pursue beloved community in their own places. I am grateful for this extended family and grateful for the opportunity I have to spend time with them whenever I travel.

This is a book that would not have been possible without the people who make my life possible. But it is, at the same time, a book. And while writing is a largely solitary activity, the making of books is not.

I want to thank the people at School for Conversion who make it possible for me to work a job where I can write most mornings: Dan, Ian, Sarah, Katelyn, Isaac, Franklin, Vern, Celia, Katie, Lauren, and Byron. The work y'all do to interrupt the school-to-prison pipeline at both the front and the back ends inspires me. Thanks for letting me tell some of the stories that your work has made possible.

I write because I don't know what I think until I see what I say. This practice keeps me sane. But it is manifestly clear to me that most of my writing would be filed away in a dusty desk drawer if not for Greg Daniel, my agent. Thanks, Greg, for helping me imagine how my words might become a book—and, what's more, a book that someone might want to read.

Every writer needs writer friends. There are no water coolers in the writer's office—no easy place to get together and talk shop. But now we have the Internet at least. Nothing boosts this writer's spirit like an e-mail with attachments from a friend who has taken time from her own manuscript to take a look at mine. Y'all know who you are. Thank you.

If these stories can be read with little effort, it is due in large part to the great effort that Ron Lee put into clarifying and refining my prose. I love to tell a story, but I still haven't mastered the English language. Thanks, Ron, for smoothing out the rough edges.

And thanks to the rest of the Crown Religion team, especially those of you who have poured your energies into this new Convergent line. It is, of course, flattering that y'all would work so hard to share my book with the world. But it tickles me even more to think about all of you working away to tell the stories of people who have so often been ignored.

I am, I admit, just the sort of ambitious, driven person who would ignore a fellow human being because I think I have something more important to do. The great gift of my adult life has been the steady presence of my wife, Leah, who could not ignore a stranger if her life depended on it. This book is, in so many ways, a testament to what I have learned from you, Leah. It's a great joy to dedicate it to you with thanks for your patience and steadfast love.

Notes

Preface

3 *being human is,* Jalal al-Din Rumi, "The Guest House," in
The Essential Rumi, trans. Coleman Barks (San Francisco:
HarperOne, 2004), 109.

4 *a guide from beyond,* Rumi, "The Guest House," 109.

4 *disguise of the poor,* Mother Teresa, *Where There Is Love,
There Is God: Her Path to Closer Union with God and
Greater Love for Others* (New York: Doubleday, 2010), 15.

5 *you just shiver,* William Stafford, "Easter Morning," in *The
Way It Is: New and Selected Poems* (St. Paul, MN: Graywolf, 1998), 6.

5 *and say carefully,* Stafford, "Easter Morning," 6.

Chapter 1

21 *left them on the streets,* Christopher Jencks, *The Homeless*
(Cambridge, MA: Harvard University Press, 1994),
46–47.

Chapter 2

33 *they shall call his name,* Isaiah 9:6; Matthew 1:23, KJV.

38 *you welcomed me,* Matthew 25:35, ESV.

38 *and you gave me,* Matthew 25:35, NIV.

54 *felt its worth,* Placide Cappeau, "O Holy Night," trans.
John S. Dwight, in *African American Heritage Hymnal:
575 Hymns, Spirituals, and Gospel Songs* (Chicago: GIA,
2001), 201.

54 *there is companionship,* Dorothy Day, *The Long Loneliness*
(San Francisco: HarperOne, 1996), 304.

Chapter 3

62 *to lay his head,* Matthew 8:20, ESV.

63 *no, not one,* Johnson Oatman Jr., "No, Not One," public
domain, in *African American Heritage Hymnal: 575 Hymns,
Spirituals, and Gospel Songs* (Chicago: GIA, 2001), 308.

63 *did it not to me,* Matthew 25:45, KJV.

65 *forever living,* Clarence Jordan, quoted in Charles Marsh,
*The Beloved Community: How Faith Shapes Social Justice,
from the Civil Rights Movement to Today* (New York: Basic
Books, 2005), 84.

Chapter 4

81 *he may devour,* 1 Peter 5:8, KJV.

86 *and synthetic passions,* Thomas Merton, *The Seven Storey
Mountain: An Autobiography of Faith* (New York: Hough-
ton Mifflin Harcourt, 1999), 148.

87 *lower than the angels,* Psalm 8:5, KJV.

87 *on sex, shopping, pornography,* These statistics are cited in
Benoit Denizet-Lewis, *America Anonymous: Eight Addicts
in Search of a Life* (New York: Simon & Schuster, 2009),
7–12.

89 *with thy might,* Ecclesiastes 9:10, KJV.

94 *who we truly are,* Kent Dunnington, *Addiction and Virtue: Beyond the Models of Disease and Choice* (Downers Grove, IL: IVP Academic, 2011), 10.

Chapter 5

100 *two-thirds of their charges,* Kenneth L. Kusmer, *Down and Out, on the Road: The Homeless in American History* (New York: Oxford University Press, 2003), 37.

Chapter 6

115 *the color line,* W. E. B. Du Bois, *The Souls of Black Folk* (New York: Dover Publications, 1994), p.v.

115 *can be judged by entering its prisons,* Fyodor Dostoevsky, quoted in Joycelyn M. Pollock, ed., *Prisons Today and Tomorrow,* 2nd ed. (Burlington, MA: Jones & Bartlett, 2005).

125 *would not the Lord see,* Lamentations 3:34–36.

126 *brings grief to my soul,* Lamentations 3:49–51.

131 *students from outside the facility,* To learn more about Project TURN, visit www.newmonasticism.org/turn.php.

Chapter 7

147 *pick up your mat and walk,* John 5:1–8.

Chapter 9

172 *the light that can shine out of a life,* Mary Oliver, "Singapore," in *House of Light* (Boston: Beacon, 1992).

177 *a younger member as an assistant,* Jonathan Wilson-Hartgrove, *The Rule of Saint Benedict: A Contemporary Paraphrase* (Brewster, MA: Paraclete, 2012), 102.

179 *the light of all,* John 1:4.

184 *middle school kids,* To learn more about Walltown Aspiring Youth (the WAY), our team-based after-school mentoring program for middle schoolers, visit www.newmonasticism .org/way.php.

Chapter 10

191 *fire shut up in my bones,* Jeremiah 20:9.

192 *why we find it difficult to wait,* Dr. Martin Luther King Jr., "Letter from Birmingham Jail," in *Why We Can't Wait* (Boston: Beacon, 2011), 88. For the full text, go to http:// mlk-kpp01.stanford.edu/index.php/resources/article /annotated_letter_from_birmingham/.

197 *building up a new world,* Sung to the tune of the Negro spiritual "We Are Climbing Jacob's Ladder." These lines became a freedom song in the black-led freedom movement of the 1960s. The song has been passed down from at least the nineteenth century, if not earlier. Civil Rights veteran and historian Dr. Vincent Harding states that the words to the song were preserved by means of oral tradition.

Postscript

199 *to walk in Jerusalem,* "I Wanna Be Ready," public domain, in *African American Heritage Hymnal: 575 Hymns, Spirituals, and Gospel Songs* (Chicago: GIA, 2001), 600.

200 *being human is,* Jalal al-Din Rumi, "The Guest House," in
The Essential Rumi, trans. Coleman Barks (San Francisco:
HarperOne, 2004), 109.

200 *compared with love in dreams,* Fyodor Dostoevsky, *The
Brothers Karamazov* (New York: Macmillan, 1922), 55,
http://books.google.com/books?id=mMNKAAAAYAAJ
&dq=dostoevsky+love+in+action&source=
gbs_navlinks_s/.

201 *I will come in and eat with that person,* Revelation 3:20.

School for Conversion works for beloved Communities that unlearn habits of social division by experimenting in a way of life with Jesus that makes surprising friendships possible. Born out of the life of Rutba House, we are building up a new world, one community at a time. Wherever you are, we invite you to partner with us through these programs.

Walltown Aspiring Youth (The WAY)
An innovative team-based mentoring program that creates networks of support for disconnected middle-school kids to cut off the supply to America's school-to-prison pipeline.

Project TURN (Transform, Unlock, ReNew)
A prison-based education program where half of the students are from outside the walls and the other half from inside, creating spaces that interrupt the dividing line of mass incarceration.

Weekend Visit
Come and experience a new monastic community where people are sharing daily life across social divisions and working for a new society in the shell of the old.

21st Century Freedom Ride
Get on board with other community-builders to learn from the wisdom of the civil rights movement and grow deeper in God's Movement today.

Learn more about all of our programs at
www.newmonasticism.org.